# HOW TO RUN A SCHOOL

Headteachers need to have a view on every possible aspect of running a school and be able to justify and articulate a set of values that tie into their vision. This essential text considers every aspect of leading a school, from the technical to the visionary, enabling you to support the best holistic educational outcomes for children.

Written by experienced Headteacher and best-selling author, Andrew Hampton, the book examines school leadership from four angles – how to lead pupils, staff, parents, and Governors. Full of practical strategies to help readers respond to the challenges and dilemmas of running a school, the chapters provide valuable insights into key topics such as inspection, behaviour, curriculum, crisis management, safeguarding, budgeting, and parent partnerships. Throughout, there is a focus on building personal and professional resilience and ways to become emotionally robust.

Written for new and aspirant Headteachers across the primary and secondary phases, as well as experienced Heads looking for fresh solutions, *How to Run a School* will enable you to hone your vision and values and project your leadership with certainty and authenticity.

**Andrew Hampton** is a former Headteacher, UK. He currently trains teachers and educational leaders in creating mutually respectful relational cultures for both boys and girls in school.

# HOW TO RUN A SCHOOL

A Manual for School Leadership

Andrew Hampton

LONDON AND NEW YORK

Designed cover image: © Getty Images

First published 2025
by Routledge
4 Park Square, Milton Park, Abingdon, Oxon OX14 4RN

and by Routledge
605 Third Avenue, New York, NY 10158

*Routledge is an imprint of the Taylor & Francis Group, an informa business*

© 2025 Andrew Hampton

The right of Andrew Hampton to be identified as author of this work has been asserted in accordance with sections 77 and 78 of the Copyright, Designs and Patents Act 1988.

All rights reserved. No part of this book may be reprinted or reproduced or utilised in any form or by any electronic, mechanical, or other means, now known or hereafter invented, including photocopying and recording, or in any information storage or retrieval system, without permission in writing from the publishers.

*Trademark notice*: Product or corporate names may be trademarks or registered trademarks, and are used only for identification and explanation without intent to infringe.

*British Library Cataloguing-in-Publication Data*
A catalogue record for this book is available from the British Library

*Library of Congress Cataloging-in-Publication Data*
Names: Hampton, Andrew, author.
Title: How to run a school : a manual for school leadership / Andrew Hampton.
Description: Abingdon, Oxon ; New York, NY : Routledge, 2025. | Includes index.
Identifiers: LCCN 2024057905 (print) | LCCN 2024057906 (ebook) | ISBN 9781032853659
 (hardback) | ISBN 9781032853604 (paperback) | ISBN 9781003517825 (ebook)
Subjects: LCSH: Educational leadership—Great Britain.
Classification: LCC LB2900.5 .H35 2025 (print) | LCC LB2900.5 (ebook) |
 DDC 371.2/070941—dc23/eng/20250220
LC record available at https://lccn.loc.gov/2024057905
LC ebook record available at https://lccn.loc.gov/2024057906

ISBN: 978-1-032-85365-9 (hbk)
ISBN: 978-1-032-85360-4 (pbk)
ISBN: 978-1-003-51782-5 (ebk)

DOI: 10.4324/9781003517825

Typeset in Interstate
by Apex CoVantage, LLC

# CONTENTS

| | |
|---|---|
| *Acknowledgements* | x |
| *Preface* | xi |

**Part I: The Headteacher** — 1

1. Who is the Headteacher? Establishing vision and values — 3
2. Vision and values – An audit and development tool — 6
3. Finding balance — 10

**Part II: Children** — 15

4. It's all about the kids — 17
5. Pupil voice — 24
6. Mental health and wellbeing of pupils — 29
7. Safeguarding — 36
8. Behaviour — 39
9. Behaviour – A personal view — 44
10. Bullying — 50
11. Policy writing — 54
12. Finding balance and working with children — 56

## Part III: Staff — 59

13 Being a unique employer — 61

14 Leadership style — 64

15 Leadership competencies — 68

16 Technology in school — 72

17 Managing teaching and the curriculum — 75

18 Managing non-teaching staff — 80

19 Money and how to use it — 82

20 School development planning — 87

21 Crisis management — 89

22 Crisis management – A case study — 91

23 Assessment and data — 95

24 Appraisal — 100

25 Finding balance and managing staff — 103

## Part IV: Parents and partnership — 107

26 Creating partnerships between parents and the school — 109

27 Dealing with complaints — 114

28 Reporting to parents — 119

29 Working with the Parent-Teacher Association — 123

30 Finding balance and working with parents — 125

## Part V: The Top Layer — 127

31 Working with the Top Layer — 129

32 Integrating the Top Layer with the school — 132

## 33  Finding balance and working with the Top Layer — 135

## 34  Fifth estate – inspectors — 137

## Part VI: Conclusion — 139

## 35  The really useful chapter — 141

## 36  Is it all worth it? – A personal summary — 144

## Postscript — 145

## 37  How to run an education system — 147

*Index* — 155

# ACKNOWLEDGEMENTS

Thank you to all the people who have helped with the drafting of this book and especially to Jenny - my wife, Naomi - my daughter, and David - my brother. I have been fortunate to work with many excellent fellow professionals in my career with whom I have shared and honed my ideas. In particular, working with Dr Jill Berry over many years has given me the confidence to consolidate my thinking about how to run a school.

# PREFACE

This book has two aims:

To challenge
To inform

## Challenge

This book contains my views on how to run a school. If you find yourself agreeing with me, then that will validate your thinking. If you disagree, then this is an opportunity to challenge your thinking with an alternative point of view.

## Inform

Running a school is a very technical task. A new or aspirant Headteacher's prior experience and study may not necessarily prepare them for the numerous things that need to be known and understood. This book aims to fill many of those knowledge gaps, some through in-depth analysis and others with a light touch.

After looking broadly at the role of the Headteacher, the book then reflects on the four 'estates' that make up a school community: pupils, staff, and parents,[1] along with Governors, Proprietors, Multi-Academy Trusts, and Local Authorities – otherwise referred to here as the 'Top Layer'. The Headteacher is uniquely positioned within the school structure. They do not sit within any of the four estates other than, perhaps, as a paid employee, which technically makes them 'staff', but not really.

Finally, I look at how we might better run an education system.

## My story

So, who *on earth* am I, and what gives me the right to write a book about education that anyone should bother to read?

I decided I wanted to be a Headteacher at around the age of 11. But the journey towards that end wasn't straightforward.

Aged 21, I got a degree in English and was about to do teacher training when exciting opportunities arose for me to work in the theatre, so I ditched the idea of teaching and became an actor/musician. After brief appearances on TV, in repertory theatre, and in the West End, I decided that acting really wasn't for me, and for a short period, I pursued a career as a commercial composer.

At the same time, I took a job as a clarinet and saxophone teacher in a fee-charging school in North London and, after six years, became Head of Music there. I have carried on composing to this day, but it gradually took second place to teaching. I then undertook lots of qualifications – gaining a licentiate in music education, a master's degree in leadership and management in education, and finally the National Professional Qualification for Headship.

I took on my first Headship at 45 and my second at 49. The second school I ran won many national awards and plaudits. I stepped away from Headship in 2021.

My career has always been in the independent sector. There is a common misconception that because independent schools usually have small class sizes and draw their pupils mostly from well-off families, everything is easy. It's not. There were many terrible events that happened to my staff, the pupils, and their parents in my school. The full gamut of horrific things happened, including suicide, rape, disappearance, incarceration, and serious injury.

The point is that I had my fair share of traumatic events. But – and it's a huge 'but' – I fully and without reservation acknowledge that the problems I encountered were never caused by poverty. It is a different matter running a large school in a deprived area where some children don't have a mattress to sleep on, where hunger is a real and present threat, and with all the other social ills that accompany economic depression. Nonetheless, the ideas I propose in this book are still universally applicable: the book is about trying to understand the daily, lived experience of each child and using that understanding to make that experience meaningful, useful, and enjoyable.

## Note

1 I am grateful to colleagues for pointing out that using the terms 'parent' or 'guardian' or 'carer' does not cover the many versions of who might be sharing accommodation and parental responsibility for children at home. The term 'grownups at home' is excellent, but for the sake of brevity, I am going to stick with 'parent'.

# Part I: The Headteacher

# 1 Who is the Headteacher? Establishing vision and values

New and aspirant Headteachers must have a view on every aspect of running a school, how they would like it to function, and what to do if things are not working. Not every new Headteacher will have achieved a complete vision for running a school as they take up their role, but the school community will expect that the values that underpin their desire and ability to do the job are in place and that those values have integrity. This and the next chapter provide a framework for some deep thinking about vision and values to help new and aspirant Headteachers get closer to being ready.

## What feeds into the Headteacher's vision and values?

Many things will feed into the new and aspirant Head's vision and values as they take shape and consolidate. The experience they had of *being* led will probably be a major influence. Candidates for Headship will probably emulate the best Headteachers they have worked with and learn lessons from the ones they felt could have been better. Having been led well or badly does not really matter – it's all helpful.

As senior teachers approach the point of applying for headships it can be useful to consider what would happen if they were given a tabula rasa: *here's a school with which you can do anything you like, nothing to hold you back; what would you do?*

## Study

Reading and study will form a significant part of preparing for Headship, and it is important to have studied pedagogy, learning, and knowledge theory, as well as being knowledgeable about every subject area. A broad knowledge of *everything* – from spreadsheets to apostrophes – is going to help decision-making, avoiding mistakes, and bringing credibility and authority to the role. The Headteacher needs to engender trust through an impressive set of competencies which are flexible, grounded in both theory and experience, and which can be applied in a universal set of circumstances.

## Autocrat or collegial leader

Though it needs to be treated as a theoretical model, it can be useful to see the decision-making style adopted by the Headteacher on a spectrum between autocrat and collegial leader. Real-life circumstances are likely to dictate that most Heads will use a mixture of collaborative sharing of decisions along with moments of clear decisiveness. However, the overall impression that the Headteacher gives will fall somewhere along this spectrum. There are advantages and disadvantages at both ends.

**At best**, an autocratic Headteacher brings a firm and unwavering vision such that everyone from the four estates can expect to know exactly where they stand and what is expected of them. Decisions are made quickly and broadcast without equivocation. Employees are partly motivated by wishing to please and be recognised by the Head.

**At worst**, an autocratic Headteacher can be accused of micromanaging and deskilling staff, leaving them unable to act autonomously. This in turn will mean more and more burden is placed on the Head, who can quickly become overwhelmed; decision-making slows down and power vacuums appear. As the Head struggles with the burden of an unworkable leadership style that they created for themselves, they start to blame others when things go wrong, creating fear and distrust throughout the school.

**At best**, a very collegiate Headteacher brings a collaborative approach to decision-making which empowers employees and develops their skills. Because decisions are made jointly, accountability is shared and a no-blame culture is established. Employees have ownership over the direction of the school and feel as if their hard work and loyalty is rewarded, which in itself is motivating.

**At worst**, a very collegiate Headteacher brings uncertainty and confusion to decision-making. It is not clear who has the ultimate say, and it feels like the Head is not taking the responsibility they are paid for. As decision-making slows, power vacuums appear which go unchallenged by the Head. Employees therefore feel uncertain about whom they should approach for a decision or to take up new opportunities. The Head tends to delegate too much and then resorts to blaming people when things go wrong.

## Blame culture

Bad versions of both autocracy or collegiality lead to blame cultures, and establishing a strong 'no-blame' culture is one of the most powerful things a new Headteacher can do. There are usually two reasons for something to go wrong:

1. The system is not working, meaning that communication has broken down or someone was overburdened and therefore overwhelmed.
2. Someone made a mistake – they forgot, or were distracted, or simply made the wrong judgement.

Either way, this is something for the Head to follow up. If the system is at fault, the Headteacher needs to change the system and take overall responsibility for making sure it works in the future. If the individual is at fault, then the Head needs to check they fully understand the system, invite some dignified contrition, and continue to offer support. A closing remark such as "We all make mistakes – myself included. Don't keep beating yourself up over this. Blame yourself once and move on"[1] can be a good way to conclude matters.

## Authenticity and integrity

Once the Headteacher's vision and values are established in their own mind and have been witnessed, actioned, and ultimately embedded into the ethos of the school, it becomes possible for the Head to lead with authenticity and integrity. Sometimes, however, external forces acting on the school can necessitate decision-making which can temporarily destabilise the established vision and values.

For instance, a Headteacher may choose to lead through a collegial sense of collaboration and empathy which permeates all levels, from senior teachers through to brand-new pupils. Faced with 24 hours to prepare for an inspection, however, orders need to be given, deadlines set with fierce consequences for failure, and time for discussion cut to the bone.

*Total* integrity in the execution of the vision and values is not possible, but each time something happens which punches a small hole in the established ethos is a moment that brings some useful realism and expediency to the way things work. Such moments, ironically, get incorporated into the vision and values – they are the exceptions that prove the rule.

## A note of caution

Research[2] has shown that some Headteachers, on appointment, completely change overnight. They lose their compassion and empathy, adopting an authoritarian, micromanaging style from day one. The research also shows that a lack of empathy being shown by senior leaders is a significant factor in poor retention of teachers across the sector.

Perhaps this is because a brand-new Head feels that now the buck stops at *their* desk, they cannot afford to trust their employees. They degrade the values that led them to Headship and adopt rigid target setting, draconian versions of classroom observations, and harsh performance management schemes. They show that their vision of leadership is closer to bullying than that of collegiality, collaboration, and community building.

This is not a good way to run a school.

## Implementing vision and values

"It's the way we do things at this school" is a powerful way of looking at the implementation of the vision and values. It works from whole school policies that define expectations of behaviour, learning, and engagement right through to how community members walk around the school, stand in the lunch queue, or behave in the playground – or, indeed, in the staff room. It is useful because it has an inbuilt resilience to challenge; if anyone wants to compare the vision and values with other local schools, or their previous experience, this statement inherently acknowledges – and at the same time denies – the comparative challenge: "Yes, I understand your comparison but . . . this is the way we do it at this school."

The statement also generates pride in the school, and pride is a powerful tool in bringing together the four estates – children, staff, parents, and the Top Layer. Each estate may feel proud of the school for different reasons, but they can all *relate* to the idea that 'this is how we do it here'. It is through the way the vision and values are embodied and manifested by the Headteacher that everyone understands what 'the way' is and how it specifically relates to them, their attitudes, behaviour, professionalism, and their relational cultures.

## Notes

1 Homer Simpson, *The Simpsons*. Season 8 Episode 6.
2 Mary Bilton, *Attrition of Mid-Career Teachers in a Neoliberal World – Why Are Experienced Teachers Leaving the Profession?*. University of Reading Institute of Education, 2022.

# 2 Vision and values – An audit and development tool

This chapter lays out 30 quick-fire questions and then ten longer scenarios that challenge current and future leaders of schools to define their vision and values.

## 30 quick-fire questions

Think about these questions hard, or just give each one a gut answer, but they must *all* be answered at some point. This list would make great preparation for a Headship interview.

### Personal style

1. Complete this sentence: "It matters to me *not* to be seen as _____."
2. Is it important that the Headteacher is liked? Yes/no/why?
3. Do you regard perfectionism as a good thing? Yes/no/why?
4. Open-door policy: yes/no/why?
5. Assemblies: formal or funky?
6. Fundamental British Values:[1] a compliance issue, or central to the ethos of the school?
7. How important is the sensory experience of the school to you, e.g. sight, sound, smell?

### Attitudes to pupils

8. Rules: kept to a minimum, or created as needed?
9. How do you aim to create opportunities for staff to discuss pupils?
10. How long is acceptable between the meetings in which every child is discussed?
11. How do you ensure that special educational needs and disability (SEND) pupils' needs are known by every teacher?
12. Rules-based or relationships-based behaviour policy?
13. Uniform: how strict is strict?
14. Detention: always needed, or aim to phase out?
15. Toilet breaks during lessons: toilet pass or trust-based?
16. Playground management: crafted to create inclusion for diversity and gender, or just free time?
17. Phones in school: yes/no, and why?

### Managing staff

18. If a member of staff had a body odour problem, would you be the one to tell them, or would you ask someone else to do it?
19. Would you give time off to a staff member who is a parent of a young child to attend the child's Nativity play or equivalent? If so, paid or unpaid?

DOI: 10.4324/9781003517825-3

20. Christmas party/Secret Santa/equivalent: are they important? Would you get involved in the organising?
21. Free tea/coffee, or contribution from staff?
22. Staff dress code: what's your view?
23. Staff Association: what does that mean to you?
24. Pay structures: stick to conventions applicable at the time, or create your own?

## Attitudes to curriculum and assessment

25. Data: do you regard hard numbers or qualitative data as more important?
26. Do you see subject areas as existing within a hierarchy of importance? Yes/no/why?
27. Would you link performance management with pay? Yes/no/why?
28. Does target setting help improve the performance of a) staff or b) pupils? Yes/no/why?
29. What is your attitude to homework: vital or mostly redundant below Key Stage 4?
30. Lesson lengths? Two-week timetable? What's your ideal?

## Scenarios that would test any Headteacher

How a new or aspirant Headteacher responds to the following ten scenarios will help define what their vision and values are. In each scenario, what should the Headteacher do?

## Scenario 1

A boy in Year 9 with severe, diagnosed and medicated attention deficit and hyper-activity disorder (ADHD) shows traits of oppositional defiance disorder from time to time. He is prone to occasional outbursts, especially when he perceives that he has been treated unfairly. His behaviour can be disruptive of other pupils' learning and many staff are keen for him to be managed into another school, be that Special or mainstream. Things come to a head when he shouts and swears at a teacher and storms out of the classroom.
What should the Headteacher do?

## Scenario 2

A mother visits a primary school with a view to applying for admission for her daughter into Reception. She is focused only on academic achievement and the potential of her daughter, who she is convinced has prodigious talent.
What should the Headteacher's response to this be?

## Scenario 3

The Finance Officer repeatedly shows a lack of competence to do the job. The Headteacher is not receiving the financial information they need and is also fielding complaints from

staff of slow throughput. However, the Finance Officer was in place before the Headteacher arrived and has the trust of the Governing Body.
What should the Headteacher do?

## Scenario 4

A group of parents with children in Year 3 start up a dialogue on the messaging application WhatsApp which is openly critical of the class teacher. The dialogue is subsequently leaked to the teacher, who is competent and experienced. The teacher is mortified and distressed and wants to resign. The union has been called.
What should the Headteacher do?

## Scenario 5

Two fathers with children at a primary school get embroiled in conflict over a minor traffic incident in the car park and end up fighting in front of other parents and their children.
What should the Headteacher do?

## Scenario 6

A Governor, new to the board, brings fresh and challenging ideas about organisational efficiency which he has successfully applied to multiple businesses. He wants the Headteacher to adopt these ideas quickly, but the Headteacher doubts that they are suitable for a school. The Chair of Governors is in two minds and refuses to take sides.
What should the Headteacher do?

## Scenario 7

A significant minority of teaching staff are refusing to hold pupils to account for breaches of the uniform rules.
What should the Headteacher do?

## Scenario 8

A group of Muslim children in Year 8 are refusing to attend assemblies in a Church of England secondary school. Their protests are supported by their parents, who are threatening to protest at the school gates.
What should the Headteacher do?

## Scenario 9

During an inspection, it is discovered that the caretaker has not been taking regular or accurate readings of legionella in the hot water system. The school is likely to be found non-compliant by the inspectorate, but the final judgement has not yet been made. What should the Headteacher do?

## Scenario 10

The school's internet system suddenly stops working. A call to the assistant Finance Officer reveals that the reason is because the bill to the internet company has not been paid. What should the Headteacher do?

All these scenarios are commonplace and are an everyday part of a Headteacher's working experience. How the Headteacher responds to each scenario will not only show the school what values they hold, but it will inform the direction the school will take as it tries to improve.

## Note

1 Fundamental British Values are democracy, the rule of law, individual liberty, mutual respect, and tolerance of those of different faiths and beliefs.

# 3  Finding balance

School leaders know that the job contains moments of stress, difficulty, and challenge. Sometimes, these moments will turn into ongoing traits that can affect the leader's ability to perform effectively in their work. To avoid this, the leader needs to manage the external adverse forces, as well as the intra-personal mechanisms needed to remain well.

It's about building strength and resilience – the ability to bounce back from adversity and not being too sensitive. It's also about nurturing in ourselves the ability to remain positive, happy, healthy, and on top of things more of the time – in a word, *thrive*. I don't want to use the expressions 'mental health' or 'emotional wellbeing' or any combination of those words because they have acquired connotations which have become confused and imprecise. Besides which, we should not ignore the many links between our *mental* health and our *physical* health; we know that we can lift our mood with exercise and diet.

What we need is *balance*.

## Getting the language right

When it comes to understanding our emotional selves, words matter.

From Brené Brown's *The Atlas of the Heart*:[1]

> "Language is the portal to meaning-making, connection, healing, learning, and self-awareness. When we don't have the language to talk about what we're experiencing, our ability to make sense of what's happening and share it with others is severely limited. Without accurate language, we struggle to get the help we need, we don't always regulate or manage our emotions and experiences in a way that allows us to move through them productively, and our self-awareness is diminished."
>
> (Preface, p. xxi)

We need to audit our feelings accurately in order to seek the help and support we need. Research quoted in Brown's book points out that it's not as easy as it sounds. Experiencing high-pressure situations will tend to diminish our ability to label our feelings and identify the effective remedies needed to regain balance.

## Stress

As an example of the power of finding the right words, let's look at 'stress'. This is a word that is often used to indicate sub-optimal conditions for thriving but is not especially precise. Here are two very different scenarios, both of which would be described as 'stressful'.

A Headteacher might feel stressed because they are in an ongoing communication with a parent whose persistent complaints are baseless. The Headteacher has tried many ways to resolve the situation, but the language directed at them is becoming personal and abusive. The Head feels bullied, though this is not something they are prepared to admit to, as they don't wish to cast themselves as a victim.

In a different scenario, the Headteacher may feel stressed because their workload has become overwhelming. They need to read and correct 120 end-of-term reports, write a Presentation Day speech, interview and appoint three new teachers, oversee next year's budget, and check next year's timetable (a pretty standard end of the summer term task list). The stress they are experiencing in this scenario comes from being overwhelmed rather than oppressed as in the previous scenario, and yet 'stressed' is the word they choose to describe how they're feeling.

When seeking support, the Headteacher may confide in someone they are close to that they are feeling stressed. But without further examination of their state of mind, their search for support is likely to elicit a form of comfort or help that doesn't necessarily alleviate the symptoms. In the first scenario - experiencing feelings of oppression - the best remedy would be the opportunity to talk it out, rant for a while if need be, and get it off their chest. Once feelings of oppression have been processed, the Head is in a better position to strategise their next actions. In the second scenario, feelings of being overwhelmed might be resolved by sifting through priorities and seeing what might usefully be delegated, then putting in some judicious overtime at the weekend - time in the office without distraction to complete tasks and reduce the overload.

Defining our terms is the first step to finding the remedy. 'Stressed' might be the term we naturally reach for, but other words can be more accurate and therefore more useful. To find the more accurate label, time needs to be taken to examine our feelings: "Am I actually feeling 'overwhelmed', or is it 'anxiety', 'fear', 'dread', 'ennui', or am I just 'emotionally enervated?'"

## Thinking patterns

We need to identify and regulate our thinking patterns. A bump in the night: is that burglars or a fox climbing under the wobbly fence panel? If the person woken by this noise is phobic about foxes, or tends to overestimate the likelihood of intruders, it will disturb their sleep. If this keeps happening and many sleepless nights are experienced, then it's time to examine how their thinking is being regulated. Some adults are not even aware that their thinking *can* be controlled and might find this concept initially strange, but it is ultimately very empowering. This is Cognitive Behaviour Therapy (CBT) at its most basic.

To control persistent and distressing negative thoughts, we need to do the following.

First realise that we are having these thoughts, they *are* persistent, and they *are* distressing. Then remember that this train of thought *can* be steered into a siding and decommissioned.

In order to silence the thought, we have to *replace* it with another one, since the brain is not capable of being thought-less for very long.

The replacement thought needs to be taken from a bank of positive thoughts, self-directives, affirmations, and mantras and hung on to until the mind has genuinely let go of the negative thoughts.

Rinse and repeat.

If you were not aware of this technique before, then perhaps research it some more. If you were aware of it but rarely if ever practise it, then perhaps this is an opportune time to re-examine how useful it can be.

Here are a few additional tips:

Many psychologists[2] and philosophers argue that the secret to happiness is *keeping your expectations low so you won't be disappointed so often*. There is something a bit cynical about that solution – positivity is equally important, in my view – but it endorses the idea that controlling one's thinking is central to balance.

The bank of positive thoughts, self-directives, affirmations, and mantras can become stale after a while, so new ones need to be found and tested.

There are countless self-help books out there, but the one that really helped me, especially in finding the most powerful and individually relevant mantras, was Robert Fritz's *The Path of Least Resistance*.[3]

## How many hours a week is appropriate and sustainable?

School is in session around 35–37 hours a week in term time, but the Headteacher is likely – along with most teaching staff – to work longer hours than that. The UK government's National Careers Service estimates a normal working week to be between 40 and 48 hours,[4] and I think that is reasonable and usually what I did. My typical working day, when there weren't any evening events to attend, would comprise 8:15am to around 5:15pm. That's 45 hours a week. I rarely worked in the evenings and hardly ever at the weekends. However, this is not an exact science, and the important thing is to achieve a working week that feels reasonably comfortable and sustainable.

A senior leader can limit their weekly hours in a variety of ways, including the following:

- Do not have access to your work emails on your phone. While many emails are innocuous and may not even need a reply, the one from a complaining parent can really upset you and flood your thinking with angst and worry. The email may arrive in the evening – they often do – but there is no need to even know about it until the next working day. If that advice doesn't suit you, then consider ensuring that new emails are not 'pushed' at you through notifications on the home screen; choose to 'pull' them instead by visiting the email app.
- Do not have access to any work files via cloud storage or virtual private network (VPN) during the evening or weekends. This limits anything you can possibly do, even when the temptation to engage with work outside school hours becomes overwhelming. It means that if you really need to work on something in the evening or weekend, you have to email yourself the documents in advance. It is planned; you are in control.
- If there is a tricky email to write, then maybe rehearse it in your head in the car and perhaps over breakfast. This mental drafting is a useful process because it means that by the time you come to write the email, you have been through the 'angry' version, the 'leave-me-alone' version, and the 'I quit' version and arrived at something that is usually balanced and to the point.

- Work efficiently. It's a good principle to try to deal with a piece of paper or email once only and not keep revisiting it. That's not entirely realistic because some correspondence requires careful thought and re-reading. By responding straight away to simple emails, you'll gain a reputation for dealing with correspondence quickly - and that helps the efficient running of the school. It can be so frustrating when all a teacher or parent needs is a quick 'okay' from the Headteacher but they have to wait 48 hours to get it.

In my experience, many senior leaders work 55-60 hours week on a regular basis. Headteachers in this position should ask themselves:

- Is this sustainable? If the pressure doesn't ease, how long can I realistically keep this up?
- What aspects of my life - like time with my partner and family - am I sacrificing?
- Given how hard I am working, what would happen if something went wrong? Like a family tragedy, or ill health? Do I have any *spare* capacity for such an eventuality?

**If the weekly workload of 55-60 hours is making you unwell, don't try to fix your mental and physical health - fix the job.**

## Sleep

Not everyone needs seven or eight hours sleep a night - I have known Heads doing just fine on far less. If you're not sleeping well and not feeling rested when you wake, then that is definitely an area of your life to focus on. First of all, if getting to sleep is the problem, then here are some tips:

- Don't work too late in the evenings. In fact, don't work at all if you possibly can - no emails, texts, or WhatsApps. Try to wind down properly and completely for at least a couple of hours before going to bed.
- It is often the case that it *feels* like you haven't slept, but actually you have. The sleep can sometimes be shallow and fitful, but it's still sleep.
- Try not to panic about not sleeping, because the adrenaline induced by the panic will make sleep less likely. Humans can survive on the odd night of sleep missed or cut short; don't make worrying about the lack of sleep a cause for the lack of sleep.
- Mantras can be very useful to help empty your mind of looping thoughts and worries. The mantra might be meaningless, like a meditative syllable. It might be just recalling a nice feeling or a moment of achievement or satisfaction. A mantra with meaning can be doubly powerful - not only do they block out troubling thoughts, they also contain a message to calm the sub-conscious. An example might be *"Let it go; you're safe."*

## Do one thing - create a *cadence of completion* each day

Keeping the evenings clear of workload is vital. Getting lost in a TV drama or documentary, or reading a novel, can bring the distraction needed to recharge. On the other hand, it might be a time to think more deeply and strategically about what is happening at school. Carrying out some research while sitting in front on the TV can be a wonderful way to stumble across ideas and solutions that would not be possible in the bustle of the working day.

In order to bring about empty evenings – and weekends – a *cadence of completion* needs to be created at the end of each working day, and especially on a Friday. The inbox is empty or marked up, the desk is clear, conversations have been had, and it's time to put down the mantle of leadership for a few hours at least. Ending each day with a cadence of completion helps to keep the burden of leadership under control.

## Notes

1  Brené Brown, *The Atlas of the Heart*. Pub Vermilion, 2021.
2  For example, https://psychcentral.com/blog/when-youre-never-satisfied-with-yourself#1
3  Robert Fritz, *The Path of Least Resistance*. Available for free at blas.com
4  https://nationalcareers.service.gov.uk/job-profiles/headteacher

# Part II: Children

# 4 It's all about the kids

As educators, we inevitably tend to see school through an **adult lens**. The way pupils view school can be dramatically different from the way adults assume they do. If we try to see school through the **pupils' lens** – understand what works and doesn't work for them – then we can re-focus our efforts to make school a more attractive experience than it currently is. We can use the mantra created by Dave Brailsford[1] in 2010 to make the GB Olympic Cycle Team the best in the world: improvement comes from the **aggregation of marginal gains**. If we can make life in school just a tiny bit better as often as possible so that pupils can look back year on year and feel the school has improved *for them* in small but noticeable ways, that in itself will encourage them to want to come to school, engage, and enjoy it. Let's start by looking at the way we encourage and try to motivate pupils.

## Rewarded meritocracy

Most schools think that to motivate pupils, you need to **reward** them. But does that work, and is it the right way to get the best from *every* pupil?

Schools habitually reward hard work, academic success, kindness, good (compliant) behaviour, effort, and sporting and cultural achievement. Rewards usually take the form of certificates, badges, handshakes, lottery tickets, and presentations during endless assemblies. It's about rewarding individual and small-group performances to promote better outcomes from the whole pupil body. But this reward system can never be truly fair, and the unfairness will always alienate and demotivate some pupils.

Pupils are also often placed in **rank order** according to their academic performance in the classroom. At the top of the rank-ordered list are – by definition – the brightest pupils, and they are consistently rewarded and validated for a gift they were born with, often whether they have worked hard or not. Again, that does not feel fair to less gifted pupils, but to compensate for this obvious unfairness, and in line with Dweck's *Growth Mindset* concept,[2] effort is recognised as well. Effort performance is not usually placed in rank order, but rewards are given to those pupils who teachers perceive have tried the hardest. This, in many teachers' eyes, levels out the playing field, gives everyone equal access to the reward system, and is therefore a 'good thing'.

Even that isn't entirely fair, though. There are three problems with judging and rewarding effort. First, it is rare that pupils with the highest attainment are also rewarded for putting in the most effort; that would just feel like all the rewards are going to same pupil every time. The effort reward seems mostly to go to pupils who have tried hard but are not the most academically gifted. The implication is that they have done well despite their relative cognitive shortcomings, so – again – not every pupil has access to this reward, and so it's not fair.

Second, it is human nature to try to get the best reward for the least amount of effort, as Black and Wiliam[3] have shown. In an assessment calibration that has A as the best mark for attainment and a scale of 1-4 for best-to-worst effort, a combined mark of A4 seems the ideal to some pupils: the very best attainment gained with the very least amount of effort. These pupils try to find subtle ways to fool the teacher into thinking they put in a lot of effort. There can therefore be a cynical reaction from some pupils when effort prizes are awarded. Pupils can think, "How do teachers know that pupil tried harder than me? Were there stated criteria against which that judgement was made, or was it just a 'feel' thing?"

Third, it is not easy for a teacher accurately to judge how much effort went into a piece of work. A pupil might have struggled long and hard over a piece of homework, finding it hard to grasp and making several false starts in arriving at the outcome. The teacher, seeing some obvious misunderstandings and a scrappy presentation, can easily make the mistake of assuming that the pupil didn't try hard enough. The result of a low effort grade can be very demotivating and upsetting for the pupil. It takes a very self-confident pupil to challenge the effort grade and ask for a review.

Adele Bates[4] cites Barrowford Primary School as going a bundle on rewards and recognition – an hour a week in celebration. Then the Headteacher asked the children what *they* thought of the reward system, and the children told her that they thought it was much more for the adults than it was for them. Consequently, the Head dropped formal rewards and redirected the time to sharing learning and inspirational moments; everyone was happier.

## Prefects, Head Girl, and Head Boy

The pinnacle of the system of motivating pupils through rewarded meritocracy is the appointment of prefects and senior pupils, such as Head Boy and Head Girl. Selecting these senior pupils from the top year group of the school – Year 6 in primary, Year 8 in a prep school, Year 11 when there's no 6th Form and Year 13 when there is – may appear to be based on merit, but defining that is actually impossible. However you try to create a fair selection process, it won't be. In one way or another, the appointment of these positions reflects **popularity**. Arguably, becoming popular with decision-makers is a skill that deserves to be rewarded, but schools just never seem to be properly mindful of those left behind.

In my own career as a Headteacher, I lamented year on year the pupils who didn't make the cut in the prefect stakes. I saw pupils doing fine in Year 11, approaching their General Certificate of Secondary Education (GCSE) studies with a steady and unwavering attitude, only to be blown off course by the announcement that they had not been made a prefect. They found it humiliating and hugely unsettling.

When it comes to being made Head Girl or Head Boy – or any variation of that – it can be a poisoned chalice. In Years 6, 8, and 11, anointed pupils find themselves having to break ranks with their peers in order to lead by example. They are obliged to be squeaky clean and never break the rules, which is not easy and doesn't always come naturally. If they do break the rules, it is not only humiliating for them but also for the senior leadership of the school because it reflects badly on the selection process. The same is true for prefects – it is so much worse if they fall foul of the rules, and their dethronement can become a massive distraction for them at precisely the moment the school expects them to be 100% focused on their studies.

Perhaps being a prefect in Year 13 might be more palatable because the pupils have reached an age when they can meaningfully contribute to the running of the school and take on the mantle of being a role model. However, by that age, many pupils are more focused on gaining the grades they need for the next stages of their lives; helping out with the cultural and logistical mechanics of their school feels irrelevant.

## Second chances

As a second chance and to give the pupils hope, the pupils who are unsuccessful in the first round of prefect appointments are set targets to achieve which will be rewarded with prefecthood after a few weeks of monitoring. Again, a huge distraction and all – for what? What is the point of prefects and senior pupils?

The arguments in favour are:

1. "This kind of meritocracy is a mirror of adult life."

    - It isn't. It would be nice to think that by working hard, obeying the law, and being good, some overarching authority figure will recognise you and place you in a position of power and superiority over your peers. But adult life ain't like that.

2. "The awarding of prefecthood and senior pupil status acts as an incentive for pupils to behave well, work hard, and attract the positive attention of the decision-makers."

    - Maybe it does incentivise some pupils, though it also makes them into a 'teacher's pet' in some people's eyes. But what damage does it do to the ones who tried really hard, understood and followed all the awarding criteria to the letter, but still didn't cross the line? How do those pupils feel about the school now? You can choose from: angry, disillusioned, alienated, cynical, oppressed, disenfranchised, overlooked, ignored and vengeful – tick all that apply!

3. "The prefects and senior pupils become role models for younger pupils."

    - Sometimes yes, but far from always, and when things don't work out, it can be damaging to the whole tone of the way pupils relate to authority. It also puts undue pressure on those pupils who – in Years 8, 11, and 13 – are still biologically driven to rebel to some extent.

4. "These pupils are useful in running the school because they can help with playground duty or regulate behaviour in the lunch queue."

    - Sounds like you're using pupils to disguise the fact that your school is under-staffed! This idea sets pupil against pupil, when they used to be friends.

5. "We have always done it like this, and our corridors are lined with the names and dates of when alumni achieved this status."

    - Well, exactly: you don't have an argument. It's just that you have never stopped to think about the downsides to all this.

As educators, we need to review how we motivate pupils and ask ourselves whether rewarded meritocracy really is the universal answer many schools assume it to be. For every reward that is given out, how is the school mitigating the potential damage to those overlooked?

If or when all the systems relating to rewarded meritocracy are removed, what is left is a school that values the intrinsic worth of learning, effort, engagement, and commitment to study. Motivation comes through the idea that success is its own reward. Pupils want to do well for *themselves*, not for a prize. Pupils are empowered to self-regulate their levels of input, effort, and performance. They are given ownership over their learning and pride generated by success is theirs. Acknowledgement by the school of their successes comes through individual interactions with staff: a smile, an encouraging comment, an enthusiastic cheer, a handshake.

*  *  *

Let's now examine some other aspects of school life and see how things might change if we view them through the lens of the pupils.

## Toilets

Toilets are a huge deal, and many children have particular sensitivities about having a poo in a space that doesn't feel private, clean, or even safe. Research by Essity[5] in 2018 found that 22% of 11-16-year-olds avoided drinking during the school day in order to avoid using the toilets, and 9% avoided eating for the same reason. From this cohort of pupils, 34% said they got headaches, 31% said they found it hard to concentrate, and 20% said it made them more irritable; 52% said the toilets were dirty, 19% described them as unsafe, 17% said the toilets were faulty, and 12% said they lacked toilet roll or hand wash. The report contains a quote from Cari, a 12-year-old girl:

> "I don't drink as much when I'm in school, I just wait until I get home. I never use the toilets at school unless I really have to as I'm worried that people will be able to hear me go to the toilet and will say something. If I do have to go, I make sure that I am as quiet as possible but that doesn't always work. It is something that I worry about a lot and would prefer to just wait until I get home to go the toilet."

Add to this the concerns some girls have with acquiring and disposing of sanitary products, and the possibility of having their first period while at school, and the picture looks grim.

If senior leaders care about the kids, then they should be checking the toilets regularly in person (after or before school). There should be a standing item on the School Council agenda to report on any issues, and all pupils should be encouraged to report any problems with functionality to the office immediately.

## Food

Pupils, especially teenagers, are often hungry; they can also be quite picky about the food they're prepared to eat. The access they have to food during the school day punctuates their experience. The quality of food at lunch is important, as is the social setting in which they eat. There is also a tension between serving food that is nutritious and food pupils like and enjoy. There are no easy wins here. If the food is worse than home, that contributes to a negative view of school and an increased sense of alienation. School leaders and people who populate the Top Layer often talk about school food with a smile and a smirk: as long as it reaches a certain minimum standard of hygiene safety and nutrition, then they think they don't need not be too concerned. Talk about 'adult lens'!

## Smell

As a Headteacher, the school I ran had a nursery. When I was showing prospective parents around the nursery, the odour from recently changed nappies was often overwhelming. No wonder pupil recruitment was poor! I determined to upgrade the facility as one of my first priorities and that included creating a separate, walled-off area for nappy changing with an industrial-strength extractor fan. I reported on this refurbishment to Governors and one remarked that in 25 years he couldn't recall ever having talked about nappies at any point. "Well, exactly," I thought.

Not only do many neurodiverse pupils have heightened sensitivity to smell, but it can make or break *anyone's* experience of a space. Typically, schools can smell of bleach – used to clean the kitchens or for washing floors, or cabbage, sweat, carpet cleaner – or simply smells emanating from poorly ventilated toilets.

If the school continues to look at these aspects of school life through the adult lens, they will fail to see that they are pivotal to the pupils' experience – but they are. That's the point.

## Liked and disliked teachers

When I was researching for my book *Working with Boys*,[6] I discovered that boys are often angry about the teachers: specifically, teachers who are boring – and that includes going too fast or going too slow.

You don't have to be liked by the pupils to be a good teacher – but you don't have to be disliked either. A pupil who is not enjoying school and is reluctant or refusing to attend will often say that they don't like some of the teachers. Some days the timetable may include only teachers who the pupil feels "don't get me." The problem is not so much that the pupil does not like the teacher but the off-putting feeling that the teacher doesn't like them. Typical remarks include "They pick on me" or "They get cross with me for no reason." The teachers who take the idea of 'tough love' too far, justifying their attitude to pupils by the results they get, need to look at themselves through the pupils' lens and see what they see then. Perhaps they need to ask themselves, as the Black Eyed Peas did, "Where is the Love?"

## Showing the love is important

Dr Andrew Curran[7] is a paediatric neurobiologist who specialises in how the brain learns. His work covers the physical changes that happen at the hormonal and cellular level and how different parts of the brain are fired up in preparation for learning to take place.

Dr Curran, when delivering his talk in front of a live audience, invites us to recall our favourite teacher from our school days. As people in the audience respond, he picks up on the common descriptors:

"My English teacher made Shakespeare come alive."
"My maths teacher always made us laugh."
"My PE [physical education] teacher made every pupil feel like they could make a contribution and that she cared how you did in her lessons."

He concludes that the one thing all these teachers have in common, the thing they all exude is . . . **love**! Dr Curran explains – though I am simplifying massively – that if the limbic brain, which is where the emotions are seated in the brain, is engaged, then dopamine is released and learning happens.

At the event of his I attended, one member of the audience objected at this point. He said, "My best teacher – perhaps not always my favourite but certainly the one who taught me the most – was my physics teacher. He was terrifying to the point of verbal brutality, but my goodness, we learnt a lot."

Dr Curran responded, "You have proved my point – emotions play a vital role in effective learning. In your case, instead of some warm, loving emotions being evoked, it was terror. It is still an emotion and it still worked."

Dr Curran proposes that teachers need to engage pupil's emotions for learning to happen effectively. He then extends this to a model of **school culture** which is effective both in promoting effective learning *and* creating respectful behaviour across the whole community. He proposes that if a child is **understood**, then their sense of **self-esteem** improves significantly. By 'understood', he means *properly* understood – in other words, understood so well that the child feels and experiences that understanding manifested through insightful comments designed to support on an individual level. Once self-esteem levels rise, the pupil starts to gain **self-confidence**. If a child feels they can fail safely and without judgement, then their learning will be bolder and more **engaged**. Engagement is the top of the tree in this model. If the pupils are engaged, emotionally and physically, then learning will happen in the most effective way across the school community.

## How can teachers 'show the love'?

Chapman and Campbell[8] have some useful ideas about how love is generally expressed and received in a variety of contexts. They argue that there are five love languages:

Physical touch
Words of affirmation
Quality time
Gifts
Acts of service

Not all of these apply to teaching! When it comes to teachers expressing approval and understanding we obviously cannot include physical touch. Gifts should be excluded from the list, too, given what we've learned about how destructive rewarded meritocracy is. However, that still leaves three: words of affirmation, quality time, and acts of service.

*Words of affirmation:* I am a firm believer that the right words delivered in the right tone at the right moment are worth a thousand certificates, badges and awards. For example, a pupil in Year 4 trips and falls over on the playground. While many children rush round to gawp, one child shows some compassionate leadership and steps through the crowd to pick up their wounded peer and take them off to the office for a swab down, antiseptic, and a plaster. The reward for that child should not be applause in front of a whole school assembly for acting out one of the school's 'Value Statements' but a quiet word in the corridor or lunch queue from a senior leader. "I heard what you did for poor Rajesh when he fell over this morning. I am really proud of you; thank you, and I appreciate your maturity and selflessness." If that doesn't validate their actions and make that child tingle with pride, I don't know what will!

*Quality time:* it's not easy when you have a class of 30 – or indeed, six classes of 30 – to find time to connect. But that's the job, and what might feel like a trivial 15 seconds of feedback and encouragement in a lesson can make a huge difference to the way a pupil feels. They feel noticed rather than overlooked or ignored.

*Acts of service:* pupils notice when marking is late or when a lesson is clearly not prepared. The act of service that shows the teacher cares is making sure they hold up their side of the teacher/pupil contract. In other words, the teacher sets work with care and thought – work that will consolidate recent teaching and also challenge and stimulate. The pupil then undertakes the work in good faith, giving the tasks their best effort. The teacher receives the work, considers it carefully and feeds back points of laudable achievement and areas for improvement, correction and further study. The pupil accepts the feedback and internalises the learning points. If the teacher breaks this chain of exchange, then it's little wonder the pupil feels let down.

This chapter has been about the importance of seeing school through the lens of the pupils and understanding how the decisions we make will be better if we do. In the next chapter, we look at the broader issue of how to discover the authentic voice of those pupils.

## Notes

1. Dave Brasilsford, https://www.bbc.co.uk/sport/olympics/19174302
2. Carol Dweck, https://caelum-online-public.s3.amazonaws.com/1504-aprenda-a-aprender/03/carol+dweck+growth+mindsets.pdf
3. Dylan Wiliam and Paul Black, *Inside the Black Box: Raising Standards Through Classroom Assessment*. Pub Kings College, London, 1998.
4. Adele Bates, *Miss, I Don't Give a Sh*t*. Pub Corwin, 2021.
5. Essity.com, https://www.essity.com/Images/Over%20half%20a%20million%20secondary%20school%20pupils%20avoid%20drinking%20at%20school_tcm339-84596.pdf
6. Andrew Hampton, *Working with Boys*. Pub Routledge, 2023.
7. Dr Curran has many YouTube videos to view, which I recommend.
8. Gary Chapman and Ross Campbell, *The 5 Love Languages of Children*. Pub Moody, 2016.

# 5 Pupil voice

There is an unspoken assumption that teaching is a bit like administering medicine to children. If the taste is not to the pupils' liking, then that's a pity – but there's not much we can do about it, and it's not going to change how we deliver it, at least not fundamentally. Schools tend to focus most of their effort on the fundamentals of teaching and learning, pupil attendance, behaviour, safeguarding, pupil wellbeing, and equality of access to learning. All these could be improved by listening more to the views of pupils and acting on them.

This is not a sentimental idea; it's not about pandering to the whims of pupils. It's about aligning an understanding of what motivates them with what we, as teachers, know we want to impart. Not every pupil is going to be happy about every aspect of school, and that's just how it is. The overall aim, however, is to create a feeling around the whole concept of being at school which is more attractive to pupils than it is unattractive. If we listen carefully and cleverly to the pupils, they will tell us how to make that happen.

Let's explore three ways in which schools currently garner the views of pupils and assess their effectiveness. Then we'll look at a new idea for how we might do this even more effectively.

## School Council

Having a School Council that meets once a week is a powerful way of demonstrating that the school regards the pupil's views as significant.

There is a clear distinction between primary and secondary School Councils. Primary Student Council meetings are sometimes dominated by an agenda of pupils wanting *more* rules and *more* punishment! There seems to be a strong desire from Year 6 pupils to contribute to a school community that is morally and ethically correct. Primary School Councils can be more useful as exercises in modelling empowerment than they are at generating insights for school improvement, though lots of exceptions to that can be found.

When working with secondary School Councils, it takes time – several years, in many cases – to raise the quality of contributions. Through regular and reliable attendance by senior leaders, pupils learn to trust that the Council is more than tokenistic. The senior leaders attending meetings must be in a position to act on decisions once they have been agreed, and not simply pass the decision up the hierarchy.

However, the existence of a School Council is far from being the only way to consult pupils. School Councils can only go so far, mostly because of the nature of the membership. As I wrote in *Working with Boys*:

> On the whole, pupils attend School Council based on one of three reasons.
> First, there are girls and boys who have chosen to be there; they want to make a difference for themselves and their peers. These pupils are often natural leaders, happy to

give up their free time in order to be rewarded by the satisfaction of a job well done, and of course, a badge.

Next, there are pupils who attend School Council because they have been picked by their form teacher who likes to give everyone in the class a turn, or at least those who have expressed a desire to represent the class; so they are there on a rota. Usually that means they don't attend for more than a few weeks before it is someone else's turn. This can mean that continuity is lost and the class's contributions and ideas fail to gain much traction. In order to make any real difference, School Council representatives usually have to push quite hard and persistently. This all takes time and effort and the rota system does not produce the best results for pupil-generated change.

Thirdly, there are pupils who, following a class vote, have been picked by their peers to represent them at the Council. This can become a form of subtle bullying. Lunchtime School Council meetings are often not what pupils would choose to attend, especially in the summer. Voting for the unpopular boy or girl to serve can be vindictive – and that is probably why many form teachers opt to make the decision on behalf of the pupils, instead of holding a vote.

(p. 37)

School Councils are needed but flawed – they contribute ideas and feedback, but their deliberations are only part of the picture.

## Surveys

A better way to garner pupils' view is through surveys. Surveys are great, but here are some tips:

1. Don't do too many: there will always be a few deliberately perverse answers from teenagers, and the more often you do surveys, the more pupils will indulge in that.
2. If comparable data is needed from surveys, they must be statistically watertight. For instance, topics need to appear in the same order in a follow-up survey as the original, with wording that matches. Don't allow pupils to opt in and out of completing the surveys – the numbers must stack up.
3. Always trial the survey first. Creating a set of survey questions is not as straightforward as you may think. It is common to complete the process only to receive pupil feedback that the questions weren't specific enough or that there was no space to add conditional comments.
4. Be careful to use words that are clearly defined so that there is no doubt or room for interpretation.
5. If you are going for multiple-choice answers, you need to decide on an even or odd number of options. I think an even number is best because if respondents have the option to 'go down the middle' – say, the third option out of five – the survey can end up producing results that don't prove much.

## Pupil tracking

This is the sort of technique that anyone outside education would see as obvious and basic – yet, we rarely do it. From time to time, why not spend a day tracking a child? That means attending every formal moment with them from registration/greeting time through all the day's lessons until the goodbye session at the end of the day. Turn on the out-of-office email alert; don't get distracted by anything; just watch and listen. There's no better way to find out what it's really like being them for a day.

As far as what the children are told, try to normalise it by saying:

> "This is called pupil tracking and senior staff do it from time to time just to find out what it's really like being a pupil in this school. Don't mind me. I'm just going to enjoy being with you all day."

There will be many reasons why an individual child or class is chosen to be tracked. There might be a mystery around why they behave well at some points of the day and not others. It may be a question of poor concentration or persistent low-level disruption. It might also be that there's a need to track a class of pupils in a troubled year group. In a secondary school, that class may not be the same pupils throughout the day, and they will probably be 'set' for maths, English, science, and modern foreign languages (MFL), but choose one nonetheless – there is much to be learned.

Looking back at my career, I didn't track pupils in this way as much I should have. When I did do it, I learned a great deal – and those days were very memorable.

## Online lives sessions

We have looked at the three most common ways of hearing pupils' views: School Council, surveys, and pupil tracking. Now let's look at a new suggestion.

Social connection is one of the primary concerns for pupils. To see school through their lens is to see their friends and peers, and the subtle shifts in the dynamics of interactions. Their world is infused with social media: the memes, the viral videos, and influencers. To have any sense of what is going on for pupils, we need to dedicate time to learning about their online lives. What pupils do when they are not at school or studying at home has changed out of all recognition in recent years.

People watch much less broadcast television than they did. Adults may still watch the news, a few dramas, and possibly even one or two soaps. What has changed significantly is the reduction in the amount of broadcast television that is watched by parent and child generations *together*. Ofcom[1] reports that while older generations are watching more streaming shows than ever before, different generations in the family home are not consuming the same content.

This has two effects. First, there is far less shared **cultural capital** between the generations than there was. Where my grown-up children and I can share quotes from *Friends*, *Pitch Perfect*, *Eastenders*, and *Love Island*, in today's families these shared cultural experiences are rarer. This is not something the younger generation are aware of, because they know no different, but it heightens the sense of disconnection between the generations and that creates more and more alienation.

Second, parents have largely given up on showing an interest in what their children are watching online. Who, over the age of 35, can name and identify the leading global influencers on the latest social media platform - say, TikTok or Instagram? Yet most 14-year-olds do know that, and they know the stories these influencers tell; they share in these influencers' online lives, and they do so with no adult support at all. For example, Sarah Shockley (@while_we.wait) has 73,000 followers on Instagram, where she tells the world the story of her ongoing battle with fertility. It is a sad story, full of hopes dashed and harsh realities faced. I heard that a group of girls in a primary school[2] were following her when she announced that her final round of in vitro fertilisation (IVF) had failed and she was facing life without having the chance of having her own children. We would normally expect children to be supported by adults when faced with a real-life narrative of trauma and tragedy like this, but no one was checking what these girls were doing online - either at home or in school.

My suggestion is to facilitate 'online lives sessions' once a week, perhaps during registration time from around Year 4 upwards. During one of these sessions, pupils in ones, twos, or threes would deliver a short presentation to the form about the things they do online. This presentation would largely be directed towards the form teacher so that they can be more informed about the online lives of the pupils in their class or form. The pupils may find this fairly challenging at first, and it might take a few goes to get the tone right, but soon they will be eager to share the best of what they have found online and start to self-regulate their behaviours too.

Does it matter that some pupils spend all their evenings watching cat videos? Not really: we're here to find out, not judge. We want to know more so we can bridge the generation gap and lessen disconnect and alienation. Young people are always likely to feel that the grown-ups don't really know their lives. Anything we can do to lessen that feeling will help.

There is, of course, an overlap here with the normal online safety talks delivered through Personal Social and Health Education (PSHE). There is an important difference between and online lives session and online safety talks. Phippen and Street[3] have researched online safety talks and have revealed some flaws. For example, teenagers are often reluctant to respond honestly to questions like "If you get into trouble online, how do you ask for help?" because they feel they either get told off or nothing is done. When asked if adults can help, teenagers say that parental overreaction is a huge problem. One said, "My father would kill the boy who shared my nude." What pupils need in relation to their online lives is a non-judgemental listening ear and some well-balanced guidance - just like we all do when faced with troubles.

Phippen and Street found pupils were most concerned by the small stuff - what the researchers call the "mundane":

> These were not specific harms, more the nagging irritation of people getting more likes for a picture or a post than someone else, or the frustration with someone maintaining a

SnapChat streak with one friend more than someone else. Issues of popularity, or what makes a good online friend, arose again and again. There was a lot of discussion about how this was the sort of thing that troubled young people on a regular, even daily, basis. They wanted to know how to deal with it but if they raised these issues with adults, they were told to "stop being so silly," or "what are you worried about that for?". What was clear was that there was little opportunity to discuss these issues in school settings.[4]

Though online safety talks may use discussion as a technique to promote learning, these lessons are still didactic in their intent. Online lives sessions, on the other hand, are non-judgemental and use guided reflection as their core pedagogical style. Teachers can discover what really worries pupils, helping them place their anxieties in context. They can also discover what excites and amuses them, so some cultural capital can be shared. Only through knowledge of this untapped world of their online lives can teachers understand the context of fallouts and fights, of wild elation and in-jokes, and the language, memes, and emojis that frame pupils' communication.

Since young people acquired access to the internet, things have changed for them – and it's time to start playing catch-up.

## Notes

1 Ofcom Survey from 2022, https://www.ofcom.org.uk/media-use-and-attitudes/media-habits-children/children-and-parents-media-use-and-attitudes-report-2022--interactive-data/
2 Information from https://esafetytraining.org know as 'The Two Johns'.
3 Andy Phippen and Louisa Street, www.headstartkernow.org.uk/digital-resilience/
4 Andy Phippen and Louisa Street, *Online Resilience and Wellbeing in Young People*. Palgrave Studies in Cyberpsychology: Springer International Publishing AG, p. 62, 2021.

# 6 Mental health and wellbeing of pupils

Several large-scale studies have shown that the mental health of teens has declined as a result of the pandemic. The question is, What should schools be doing about that?

In *What Mental Illness Really Is . . . (and What It Isn't)*, Lucy Foulkes[1] tells the history of how, in 2007, mental health and wellbeing became the topic of wide public discourse and numerous awareness-raising campaigns, led by celebrities such as Ruby Wax and Stephen Fry. A few years later, the Duke and Duchess of Cambridge, as they were then, got involved. But awareness is one thing, and understanding what to do about children's mental health issues is another.

There have been unintended consequences resulting from these ongoing campaigns. Foulkes writes, "In the rush to destigmatise mental illness . . . all kinds of normal negative emotions and experiences are being labelled as mental disorders – or at the very least, as problems that need to be instantly fixed" (p. 7). Foulkes and others have published research which points at the potential damage being done by mental health and wellbeing programmes and interventions in school. How, they ask, do we know whether the hotchpotch of programmes being delivered in schools are actually making things better rather than worse?

Mental distress and diagnosable mental illness exist on a spectrum, influenced by biological, psychological, and social factors. It is important that we don't allow 'diagnostic creep' but instead distinguish between what is a condition requiring specialist treatment and what is an expected human reaction or 'reactive distress'. A teenager experiencing 'the blues' because of repetitive episodes of unrequited love is not necessarily depressed, even though their symptoms of tearfulness and lethargy seem to overlap with a diagnosis of depression. An 8-year-old who experiments with refusing certain foods is not necessarily anorexic. A 6-year-old who struggles to sit still and concentrate does not necessarily have ADHD. A danger exists that with greater mental health awareness, we are pathologising aspects of the adolescent experience.

## Pathologising unhappiness

As John Stuart Mill[2] said, "Ask yourself if you are happy and you cease to be so." This is especially true for children. Children have very little agency in the way they run their lives, something that has intensified for recent generations. They are inevitably prone to the circumstances of their social, physical, economic, and cultural environment, with little opportunity to remove themselves from difficulties. The circumstantial hardships being imposed upon them affect their thinking patterns, and unhappiness can follow. But where negative circumstantial factors are negligible, we must guard against making children unhappy through suggestion – and that can be the unintended consequence of awareness-raising programmes. **We have to be very careful not to pathologise the normal negative feelings that every human can expect to experience.**

It is still the case, of course, that some children need professional interventions to deal with their unhappiness.

## The mind is situated

We should not see the child's mind and its symptoms as 'stand-alone'. A child's mind is a cognising agent upon which all the forces of every waking and sleeping moment are acting. Some psychiatrists view as anomalous the model of diagnosing and then treating a child experiencing symptoms of mental ill health because the child's mind is not a fixed single entity, in and of itself.

Phippen and Street's research[3] has unpicked the forces acting upon the young person's mind. They deconstruct this into the following five areas:

- Microsystem: the child's immediate environment, such as home, family, and close friends.
- Exosystem: people who and places that have an indirect impact on the child's life, such as their wider community, formal and informal education settings, social care, healthcare settings, etc.
- Macrosystem: government policies and cultural values, including laws, social values, and economic drivers.
- Chronosystem: the influence of change and constancy in a child's environment, acknowledging that the child's environment, and influences, will change over time.
- Mesosystem: different parts of the child's immediate environment interacting together.

This deconstruction is useful in showing how we need to see the mind as situated in its social context. It seems logical to conclude that the post-pandemic increase in teen mental illness has been largely driven by changes in social systems, and that is where schools can make a difference. The analysis justifies building a whole school policy for mental health and wellbeing based on a holistic approach.

## Building a comprehensive whole-school policy for mental health and wellbeing

A whole-school policy needs to cover the following three bases:

1. **Mental health awareness education:** making pupils aware of how they can make good lifestyle choices to ensure they remain mentally healthy.
2. **Coordinate reactive support for pupils experiencing significant distress or potentially diagnosable mental disorders:** this includes systems of monitoring, recording, and assessing, along with providing training for an appropriate level of school-based support and access to professional expertise.
3. **Improve pupils' wellbeing by making school somewhere they want to be:** apply a range of strategies that fulfil children's need for good social connection, a pleasant environment, motivational encouragement, recognition of their individual selves, mutual respect, and fairness. In totality, we might label these strategies 'system therapies' – i.e., therapy that is applied across the whole system.

These bases are described in more detail in what follows.

## Mental health awareness education

There are many excellent schemes promoted by organisations like the PSHE Association, Young Minds, and The Wellbeing Hub, but each one needs to be checked for the risk of pathologising normal levels of unhappiness.

Here are some quick suggestions and ideas to strengthen mental health awareness education:

- Teachers need to ensure the topic of mental health is presented in ways the pupils find relatable and not through an adult lens. In her work in schools, Australian researcher Dr Alexandra Marinucci[4] found that much of this subject matter, when presented in the wrong way, was ridiculed by pupils who felt patronised by adult interventions.
- An important topic to cover is the daily routine and habits of pupils. To discover more about the lived experience of pupils, it can be helpful to perform regular **audits of online habits**. In the last chapter, I suggested making time to explore pupils' online lives so that the generational divide is bridged to some extent by shared cultural experiences. It is equally useful to discover how much time boys and girls spend online and how that affects their **sleep**. There is, in my experience, an alarming misconception in the minds of many secondary age pupils that sleep doesn't matter and is not as important as continued social engagement. Similarly, they don't regard **breakfast** as important, either – yet every mental health expert will tell them that both are highly significant in maintaining wellbeing and happiness through an inherently challenging period of their lives. It is therefore vital that due emphasis is given to sleep and breakfast.
- Choosing the **right people** to deliver this topic is important, and I suggest that form tutors (secondary) or class teachers (primary) are not always best placed to do this. Good strategies to maintain wellbeing need to be taught by staff who are adept, trained, and willing.
- Gemma Marks[5] writes about the issue of **solo-rumination** and defines it as repeatedly and persistently thinking about one's problems, concerns, or negative emotions in solitude. It involves a self-reflective and introspective focus on personal experiences, thoughts, and feelings without external input or interaction with others. Those who promote mindfulness as a technique to promote wellbeing need to warn pupils of the dangers of solo-rumination. Mindfulness needs to be guided and coached to avoid this.
- **'Contagion'** has unfortunate connotations, but the word is generally used to describe the way in which some forms of mental illness such as suicidal ideation, gender dysphoria, anorexia, and self-harm can cluster within a cohort in a school. The need and desire to blend in can be felt keenly amongst children and adolescents, and contagion is something to be aware of.
- Some schools that give time over to 'character education' and, as part of that, encourage pupils to discover and then project their **authentic selves**. Though this is laudable in some ways, we need to keep in mind the need for both boys and girls to fit in and blend. The imperatives of strong social connections can far outweigh their desire to present their authentic selves to the world, and care needs to be taken in promoting this idea.

- Mental Health Week, Anti-Bullying Week, Pride Month, and other themed time periods are all examples of society-wide mechanisms designed to raise awareness of various issues. The problem with these **special 'weeks'** can be that they confine the topics to five school days and seem, in some cases, to remove the obligation to take those topics seriously for the other 51 weeks of the year. There can be some rather cynical or lazy thinking which goes: *"We did Mental Health Week and we did Anti-Bullying Week, so the pupils should not be experiencing poor mental health and are not being bullied, right?"*

### *Coordinating reactive support for pupils experiencing potentially diagnosable mental disorders*

The tracking of pupils' mental health tends to be different in every school. The challenge for the leadership team is to find ways in which individual pupils can be discussed by staff who know that young person from different perspectives. An ideal team of people might include someone from the SEND department (if relevant), a form tutor, and a senior lead – whether that's the Head of Year or a pastoral leader.

Many schools keep extensive digital records of concerns about individual pupils. However, it is easy for the staff who monitor the concern-recording platform to become overwhelmed by the sheer volume of posts, so capacity and clear systems are vital to prevent pupils falling through the net.

The Mental Health and Wellbeing Policy needs to outline ways in which the school will work with parents to facilitate access to appropriate diagnoses and treatment.

### *Improve pupils' wellbeing by making school somewhere they want to be; focus on high quality relational cultures*

If we can make school a more attractive place where pupils feel safe and can enjoy themselves, then overall levels of happiness will improve. There is a balance to be struck between spending financial resources on mental health support professionals and spending money on improving the daily experience of pupils. We can recall and repeat here the mantra, which I proposed in Chapter 5: it's all about improvement through the **aggregation of marginal gains**. If we can make life in school just a tiny bit better as often as possible so that pupils can look back year on year and feel the school has improved for them in small but noticeable ways, that in itself will encourage them to want to come to school and enjoy it.

Every gain – however small – is worth more than the thing itself, because each gain is an indication that the leaders of the school want to make things better, to offer more, to listen and respond more, to empower more, and understand more. This is the path to pupils' happiness.

A meta-analysis by CHConline.org[6] of research into pupil happiness in schools showed that the biggest factor was good social connections. When pupils come home from school, they are less interested in sharing their learning than they are in talking about what happened between them and their friends. Schools want pupils to be good friends, and a small amount of curriculum time is given over to this. However, high-quality relational cultures come a poor second to other priorities – such as exam results and compliance with school rules. For most pupils, relationships with peers are central to their happiness, and if those relationships are trusting and reliable, then the school's priorities are much more likely to be achieved. The policy needs to focus on supporting pupils to build relational cultures that are consistently mutually respectful.

Relational cultures may refer to peer-to-peer relationships, but it is also vital to build a teacher-to-pupil culture which fosters open, mutually respectful interaction. Patronising and controlling behaviour from teachers is likely to worsen the psychosocial factors affecting mental health outlined earlier, including teenagers' sense of having little autonomy and being misunderstood. Pre-emptively strict lectures or sweeping statements about "how disappointing Year 9's behaviour has been" will work against building a culture of trust and resilience.

Boys and girls can, of course, be friends with each other, but on the whole, girls and boys form friendships in different ways. A gendered approach to friendship is not something everyone feels comfortable with, but if you ask the pupils themselves, they will agree that girls' and boys' friendships are not better or worse – but they are different.

As a Headteacher, I developed two strategies to support the relational cultures of pupils – *Girls on Board* and *Working with Boys* – using an empathy-based approach and delivered through guided reflection.

## Girls

I founded **Girls on Board**[7] in 2017 in response to girls falling out badly and leaving the school that I ran. The fallouts were happening so frequently that I had no choice but to find a different way to support the girls. My research led me to Rosalind Wiseman's book *Queen Bees and Wannabees*,[8] and her ideas helped me create an approach which empowers girls to navigate the choppy waters of friendships for themselves. If you ask a group of girls whether things get better or worse when grown-ups get involved in their friendship issues, they will reliably and with some vehemence tell you they get worse. That is because, when faced with unhappiness caused by friendship turbulence, a teacher's instinct is to interview and probe. The teacher's investigations aim to find the truth so that they can apportion blame. But that technique rarely works. The truth is never simple, accused girls rarely admit culpability, and ... things get worse. Girls are accused of snitching, parents get angry and start complaints about bullying, and huge amounts of time are consumed. Nor does restorative practice work, because the girls won't want to be entirely honest in front of a teacher; 'resolutions' are usually tokenistic and agreed upon just to get out of the room.

More than 1,000 schools across the world have adopted the *Girls on Board* approach which supports girls and their friendships through sessions which are designed to evoke empathy – and lots of it. Through discussions of relatable dilemmas and scenarios, the girls realise they have huge amounts in common when it comes to anxiety about trusting and reliable friendships. The consistent application of the *Girls on Board* approach leads to more harmonious friendships amongst the girls, who also learn a lot about conflict resolution and how to let go of grudges. It also reduces instances of bullying and helps re-establish friendships in the aftermath of bullying.

Those 1,000-plus schools will attest to the fact that it works. We have to ask: how many girls are not attending school today (or are very reluctant) because they don't feel they have trusting and reliable friendships? I suspect it is a very high percentage, and even those who cite other reasons are very possibly covering up the real reason – friendship – because the adults in their lives don't regard 'friendship' as a good reason not to attend school.

## Boys

In 2023 I wrote *Working with Boys – Creating Cultures of Mutual Respect in Schools*.[9] The scope of the book is wider than just friendship and holds up a mirror to life in general as a boy in school – especially aged 9 and older. The aim is to prompt boys to form relational cultures that work for everyone, choosing as their common values compassion, consideration, respect, and dignity rather than opting to be harsh, over-competitive, and cruel and indulge in sexualised banter. *Working with Boys* is a programme of 13 lessons designed to be delivered through PSHE at a crucial time in boys' psychological development – age 11, at the beginning of Year 7. That is when boys decide on the version of masculinity they are going to adopt for themselves as individuals. As each boy develops a personal identity, so the rules that define the cohort's relational culture take shape. Once the relational culture has been adopted – by the end of Year 7 – it is extremely hard to change it. That is why it is so important to work with the boys, and with the girls' help and support, to form a way of relating to that is gentle. The relational culture is defined by the boys' reaction when something happens:

- Someone scores an own goal minutes before the end of a crucial football match: do his teammates berate him or comfort him?
- A boy makes a pornographic remark about a female teacher: do the boys laugh or frown?
- A boy's family dog dies and he is in tears: do his peers mock him or comfort him?
- A boy starts to abuse a girl in his year group with inappropriate touching and language. Do his peers ignore him or report him?

The schools that have adopted the *Working with Boys* programme have seen a reduction in harmful sexual behaviour, and cohorts of boys and girls passing through the school consistently showing mutual respect.

Both *Working with Boys* and *Girls on Board* use guided reflection as their pedagogical style. As we saw in the chapter on Pupil Voice (Chapter 5), relatability is key. This is about the adults having empathy for the pupils, seeing school life as they see it, and working with their imperatives rather than choosing to ignore them. This is not about pandering to the whims of the young; this is about understanding what drives their thoughts and actions, what motivates them, what makes them happy, and what makes them unhappy.

In terms of mental health and wellbeing, *Working with Boys* and *Girls on Board* are system therapies, working to address the negatives and reinforce the positives by using empathy as central driver.

## Summary

The best way to run a school is to acknowledge that some pupils will experience poor mental health and do whatever you can to support them in changing that. However, simply making the school the best experience for pupils will always be the most effective strategy to increase overall happiness. Creating that best experience includes understanding that pupils of all ages will have low moments – and in adolescence in particular, that is entirely normal and to be expected. Of all the strategies that can be deployed to help, prioritising mutually respectful relational cultures will reap the most rewards.

**Notes**

1 Lucy Foulkes, *What Mental Illness Really Is . . . (and What It Isn't)*. Pub Vintage, 2022.
2 John Stuart Mill, *Autobiography*. Longmans, Green, Reader, & Dyer, p. 100, 1873. Oxford University Press, Oxford, 2018.
3 Andy Phippen and Louisa Street, *Online Resilience and Wellbeing in Young People*. Pub Palgrave Macmillan, 2002.
4 Alexandra Marinucci, *The Need for Mental Health Education in Australian Schools*. Pub University of Monash, 2021.
5 Gemma Marks, 'Parent and Teen Conversations'. Marks regularly posts on LinkedIn about teenagers and their mental health.
6 A huge online resource dedicated to children Mental Health, https://www.chconline.org/resourcelibrary/how-to-be-happy-according-to-science/
7 GirlsonBoard.co.uk
8 Rosalind Wiseman, *Queen Bees & Wannabes: Helping Your Daughter Survive Cliques, Gossip, Boyfriends, and New Realities of Girl World*. Pub Harmony Book, 2009.
9 Andrew Hampton, *Working with Boys – Creating Cultures of Mutual Respect in Schools*. Pub Routledge, 2023.

# 7 Safeguarding

**(The thoughts and ideas in this chapter are not a substitute for a thorough and grounded knowledge and understanding of statutory safeguarding guidance.)**

Statutory guidance from government has grown in volume and complexity over the last 20 years – so much that the responsibility for safeguarding pupils, and all members of the school community, has become very difficult to manage. While schools have significantly expanded their provision to safeguard pupils, the extra-mural services – such as psychological, psychiatric, speech and language, and SEND diagnostic support – have not kept pace.

KCSiE[1] is the most significant of the many guidance documents issued by government to keep children safe. It defines safeguarding as "taking action that promotes the best outcomes of all children." Every year, KCSiE is revised and new sections and paragraphs are added. A close examination of KCSiE in 2023 reveals that, in addition to its 166 pages, there are 77 recommended websites to visit for more information, and over 2,100 pages contained in downloadable portable document files (PDFs). It is hard to believe that even the most proficient safeguarding professional has read all this material, or could boast a comprehensive recall of every detail.

The guidance has become so complex that you could argue that it is – very ironically – not clear enough to be safe. For example, I have visited hundreds of schools in the last few years in my capacity as a trainer of teachers, and I have found that, despite all those thousands of pages of guidance, the interpretation and application of safeguarding protocols for visitors is inconsistent. In some schools, I am free to wander unaccompanied down a corridor with a red visitor's lanyard with no ID, yet in other schools my photo ID and DBS[2] are checked and recorded, and I am accompanied by a staff member for every moment of the day.

## Battling against the 'myth of more'

The principle seems to be that more words within a policy will make us safer, and more training on safety measures will reduce the incidents of harm. Maybe that's true, but what are the unintended consequences?

The labour costs involved in safeguarding interventions are substantial – every school has a Designated Safeguarding Lead (DSL) and that person is usually a Deputy Head. The DSL often spends several hours a week on safeguarding issues, and that has a knock-on effect on their ability to perform other senior leadership duties; so, more Assistant Heads are employed – it all costs money. School budgets have not expanded to meet the additional needs of safeguarding, meaning that schools have less money to spend on everything else.

Another unintended consequence of safeguarding is felt in the loss of freedom for pupils and staff. The security arrangements in some schools are oppressive and feel like you are entering a prison – guarding a precious and vulnerable set of inmates from predators who may come from any walk of life and attack at any moment. So I ask: how far has our extreme aversion to risk caused greater levels of anxiety in pupils, de-skilled everyone in the school community, and promoted learned helplessness in children?

## Using risk assessments to enhance the response to safeguarding concerns

Safeguarding is focused on safety and is therefore an extension of the conceptual edifice of 'Health and Safety'. Over the years, society has honed its ability to root out unsafe practices in every walk of life and make things safer.[3] There are fewer people falling off ladders or being maimed or killed in relatively minor car accidents. But even the most zealous health and safety expert would admit that there is a diminishing rate of return. It is not possible to make all aspects of life entirely safe, and that's why we have risk assessments – to understand how we can mitigate risk and reduce harm. A good risk assessment will always consider the unintended consequences of mitigations, and that is something schools could do better.

In relation to safeguarding, we need a more calibrated and triaged approach. KCSiE already recommends a three-step response, with early identification and intervention leading to escalation of concerns and finally multi-agency cooperation. However, it is in the first stage – early identification and intervention – that DSLs, understandably, tend to over-react for fear of being accused, later on, of under-reacting. There is no reason why an individual school shouldn't take the opportunity to create a new labelling system that sits within the umbrella of safeguarding but that allows practitioners to calibrate the seriousness of the concern being raised. In particular, a risk assessment should be the initial response to *every* report of a safeguarding concern and on the risk assessment pro-forma should be the question, "What are the potential unintended consequences of every possible planned intervention?"

## Scenarios

Let's look at a safeguarding scenario and see how a risk assessment approach might help.

One of the most common safeguarding issues facing DSLs is reports of sexting – the practice of sending and receiving pictures of naked genitalia – or 'nudes', as they are referred to. A pupil in receipt of an unsolicited 'nude' has an awkward judgement to make in deciding whether to report the incident to the school. The pupil risks being accused of being a snitch and being ostracised. The consequences of reporting the incident might be severe for the perpetrator: the creation and digital transmission of obscene images of a person younger than 18 is deemed by law to be the creation and distribution of child pornography; on the other hand, the victim might justifiably be shocked and angry and want the perpetrator sanctioned and made to stop. It is a dilemma.

If the victim does decide to report the incident, there are also dilemmas for the school. The DSL needs to consider the best way to achieve the ongoing safety of both the victim and the perpetrator. They also need to consider the effects any actions may have on the relational cultures between pupils in the school. At the same time, they need to maintain the trust of parents and limit potential damage to the school's reputation. The careful consideration of all these factors may result in a judgement that does not please everyone, but the completion of the risk assessment ensures that the thinking is recorded and justified.

## The prevention curriculum

Schools put a lot of thought into lessons and assemblies that focus on keeping pupils safe in both the real and digital worlds. In primary schools, it is appropriate to *teach* pupils how to be safe, to warn them of danger and how to recognise it and therefore avoid it. Teenagers, however, can be counter-suggestive, and messages are far more effectively delivered using guided reflection as the pedagogical style.

For instance, a good way to discourage sexting is not to over-emphasise the illegality of the practice but to guide pupils to reflect empathetically on how violating and traumatising it can be to receive when unsolicited. The reality is that local police forces are very reluctant to criminalise teenagers for these activities, and the best way to prevent it from happening is to promote self-regulation. **The curriculum needs to focus on the dignity and power of self-control, looking at the benefits of mutually respectful behaviour for both the individual and cohort.**

Safeguarding has become a permanent part of running a school, and statutory guidance will no doubt continue to grow in volume and complexity. That doesn't mean that the people running the school should not consider carefully how to safeguard the school community in the most *efficient* way and apply strategies that minimise cost and unintended consequences. Above all, DSLs need to calibrate, triage, and identify what is and what is not a safeguarding issue – and have the confidence to trust their judgement.

## Notes

1 Keeping Children Safe in Education.
2 Disclosure and Barring Service.
3 www.rsph.org.uk/our-work/policy/top-20-public-health-achievements-of-the-21st-century.html

# 8 Behaviour

No aspect of running a school reflects the Headteacher's values more than the way the behaviour of pupils is managed. In undertaking any serious review of behaviour management policies, the Headteacher has to ask: "Do the pupils behave well because they are obliged to, or because they want to?" Some Heads will argue that it doesn't matter either way, as long as they behave – but is that sustainable?

## The spectrum of discourse

The public discourse on how to regulate pupil behaviour has been characterised by polarisation, mostly between 'rules-based' and 'restorative' – or 'hard' and 'soft', respectively. As we might expect, the extreme ends of this spectrum can lead to absurdities. The discourse has been largely unhelpful, leading to division amongst professionals. It has let down pupils and parents and left them feeling that something as fundamental as behaviour management should not be so controversial or inconsistent between schools.

## The 'hard' end

At the 'hard' end of the spectrum, pupil behaviour is managed through a rule-based policy which is adhered to strictly and rigidly. The policy lays out examples of behaviour that are proscribed, and a tariff is attached to each one.

'Hard', rule-based, behaviour policies tend to be lengthy because there is a need to cover every type of behaviour deemed sanctionable. This 'list of sin' will necessarily cover things such as uniform, homework completion, swearing, corridor flow, toilet attendance, respect for others and their possessions, preparedness for lessons by having the right equipment, and so on. The more mature the policy, the longer the list of sin. It might have some positive things to say about high expectations but is largely focused on negative forms of conduct.

The problem with rules-based behaviour policies is that they can be too rigid. It's all very well to use expressions like 'zero tolerance', but it precludes the opportunity to use common sense. For example, if there is zero tolerance for anyone *ever* speaking during the taking of the register, then when someone gets a nosebleed but can't interrupt to access a tissue, they end up bleeding all over the desk. Zero tolerance de-skills the pupils, taking away their agency and levelling down any sense that they might be trusted to do the right thing.

One of the strongest arguments for rigid rules is that they are fair – everyone is held to account under the same regime. But rigidity is far from fair, as the Equality Act 2010 painstakingly explains. Pupils with protected characteristics, including SEND, are entitled to *reasonable adjustment* – and that immediately makes 'zero tolerance' untenable.

Not only that, but rigidity is also the enemy of self-regulated harmony. It reduces opportunity for autonomous, self-correcting decision-making; it infantilises the pupils and reduces them to programmable robots. Pupils become fearfully compliant rather than willingly obedient and respectful of authority.

## The 'soft' end

So, what of the 'soft' end of the spectrum? This is sometimes characterised by the replacement of a Behaviour Policy with a 'Relationships Policy'. Behaviour is managed through the demand for mutually respectful relationships – though the emphasis is often on respect being shown *by* students *to* teachers, rather than the other way round. A focus on the quality of relationships *between pupils* is often absent, apart from an over-reliance on 'kindness' as a cure-all.

At the heart of many relationships policies is the strategy of 'restorative conversations' (also known as restorative practice and restorative justice). Sanctions are replaced by conversations which seek to restore respect by guiding pupils to reflect on their poor judgement and, if necessary, apologise. The obvious problem with this policy, which supporters of the rule-based approach are quick to point out, is that when a pupil has just thrown a chair at you, told you to "f*** off," and stormed out of the room vowing to make his own way home, the response of a 'restorative conversation' feels a bit limp.

The problem with the 'restorative' approach is that a) it is often universally applied when in reality there are only very specific circumstances when it is appropriate and effective and b) the word 'restorative' has come to be associated with behaviour policies that are too soft and not effective.

However, the strategy of holding the poor behaviour of a pupil to account through a conversation can be very effective – I just think we should label it simply, '**a talk with** . . . [the Headteacher/Deputy Head, etc.]', and it should not necessarily always end with 'restoration'. Sometimes the 'talk with . . . ' needs to be just that, and the pupil is left to reflect in their own time. The 'talk with . . . ' is not framed by policy or given strategic aims or expected outcomes because that just constrains the process. The 'talk with . . . ' is a chance for the senior leader to hold the pupil to account with opening remarks, such as "What on earth did you think you were doing?" or "What's going on with you?" or "Tell me what actually happened." The tone of the senior leader is exacting and relentless. There is room for compassion and forgiveness, as well as explanations of what the reasonable next steps might be. The pupil is treated as entirely capable of contrition, remorse, apology, and self-correction, even if it takes some pressure to get to that point.

If you treat a recidivist as a recidivist, they will continue to be one; if you treat them with conditional generosity, you give them the chance to self-correct.

## Mind the gaps

To make sense of both the 'rules-based' and 'restorative' approaches, we need to fill in two gaps in the thinking.

First, we need to examine the **purpose** of the sanctions contained in the Behaviour Policy. Does the 'stick' part of a 'carrot and stick' approach actually lead to the behaviour we aim for, or do we need a policy that is more nuanced?

Whatever the nature of an incident of poor behaviour, whether very minor or extremely serious, the desired outcome of adult intervention is not in dispute; we all want the following:

- The incident dealt with fairly.
- The perpetrators to learn from their mistakes and be deterred from repeating them.
- The perpetrators to apologise if appropriate and deliver reparations if necessary.
- The possible victim(s) – sometimes that means 'the school' and its reputation – vindicated and acknowledged.
- For justice, as witnessed by the community, to be seen as having been done.

The need to be consistent in our interventions with pupils needs to focus on these five bullet points. This then allows for merited leniency and mercy. Contrition, remorse, and circumstance all need to play into the final consideration of an intervention, even if the outcome appears anomalous compared to parallel incidents. **The punishment shouldn't fit the crime; it should fit the situation.** The Headteacher's office is not a court of law; pupils are not criminals – unless and until they have been found guilty in a court of law. They are children making mistakes and finding their way.

Second, we need to **calibrate** behaviours so that we can make common-sense distinctions between the mildly anti-social, annoyingly impertinent, self-consciously recidivistic, and downright violent. Only then can we create a behaviour strategy that works for everyone, which underpins a community cohesion where everyone feels safe and acknowledged. If we can get this right, then the rewards are huge. To reap the benefits of such a policy is to create an environment where all community members can thrive in a mutually supportive relational culture which empowers and entitles everyone to be the best version of themselves.

## Calibrating behaviours

Useful calibration of behaviours does not just involve taking entries on the list of sin and putting them into categories. Calibration should be fluid and allow for context. To illustrate this, let's see what happens if we classify misbehaviour into 'serious', 'moderate', and 'mild' categories.

**Seriously** bad behaviour would be classified as anything that breaks the law – being violent or dangerous, damaging property, making serious threats, sexual misconduct, and bullying. Putting this behaviour in the context of the law at this point doesn't mean the school needs to involve the police. There are plenty of things that happen in schools which, if reported, would oblige the police to investigate. The police and the Crown Prosecution Service (CPS) are naturally and understandably very reluctant to criminalise children, but it is useful to match an instance of seriously poor behaviour against whichever law has hypothetically been broken to see if this classification fits. Once an incident has been classified as serious, it is important to take context into consideration. As with the law, consideration of mitigating circumstances is needed because they will necessarily affect the outcome in terms of sanctions delivered.

**Moderately** bad behaviour – to give it a rather lazy definition – sits between the serious and the mild. It's not serious, though it might become so if it carries on. Neither is it mild. It needs addressing in such a way that the pupil is in no doubt that lines have been crossed, that behaviour needs to improve, and that records have been kept.

**Mildly** bad behaviour is often the result of pupils' over-excitement or lazy choices. It needs addressing but not in a way that is oppressive or over-reactive. A Year 7 is running down a corridor and is called back by a teacher. As you watch the teacher gently admonish the pupil, you see on the pupil's face that they don't want to be in trouble. This is embarrassing, and they feel a little shame and disappointment in their own behaviour. In other words, the teacher need not do much more than a stern look and eyebrow raised in earnest. That might not be true of a pupil in Year 9 where their sheer size becomes more intimidating and hazardous. If this incident has become typical of this pupil's behaviour, it starts to border on **moderate**.

This may seem obvious, and a common-sense approach. It is the instinct of most teachers to categorise behaviour in the moment – a judgement they usually get right and inevitably sometimes get wrong. The Behaviour Policy should support those judgements of when to be lenient, and when to avoid humiliating a pupil – giving them the chance to restore respect without resorting to the tariff-based sanction system and the list of sin.

## Relationships

The idea that overall levels of behaviour will improve when the relationships between people in the school improve is widely – though not universally – accepted. In *When the Adults Change, Everything Changes*,[1] Paul Dix argues that if the teachers show pupils respect and build trusting relationships by being consistent, positive, and fair, then profound improvements follow. It's hard to disagree with that, though bringing *every* teacher on board takes time and commitment from the leadership team. Schools can go much further if they focus, as well, on the relationships between pupils. Therefore, the application of the *Girls on Board* and *Working with Boys* approaches – both based on the evocation of empathy – is as significant a strategy in improving behaviour as anything imposed by a sanctions policy.

## Using respect as a behaviour management tool

If you give bucket loads of respect to your pupils, you will get at least *some* of that back. This is a relentless and effortful process which, depending on your starting point, can take time. Respect is shown through the granular moments in the corridors – a smile, a greeting, a remembered conversation, a quip designed to acknowledge and validate. Respect is also gained through a rational and compassionate interpretation of the Behaviour Policy. The accumulation of granular moments builds trust and a genuine sense that the school wants to do the right thing. To some pupils, 'school' and 'teachers' will always be 'the enemy' because they represent authority, but these pupils will give the school respect if enough is shown towards them. You can just hear a teenager saying, "I hate school and you'll never change that, but when you let some of us inside at break times because it's really cold – yeah – respect for that."

Respect, once established, will breed trust, and trust will improve attitudes and behaviour. The conditional withdrawal of respect then becomes a lever - part of the 'stick' of 'carrot and stick'. If a pupil behaves moderately or seriously badly, they find themselves sitting in front of senior leaders with a look of disapproval and disappointment on their faces. Even the 'hardest' teenager will notice that; it hurts, and they want to regain the leader's respect and approval.

You may think that's soft, but it's not. It's exacting, and it holds the pupil to account for what they have done. Whatever their familial, environmental, financial, social, or psychological circumstances, they want and need affiliation with the community, and through your words and body language, you are threatening to take that away. Being grilled by a senior teacher whose eyes are burning into theirs is a lot more uncomfortable than spending time on their own in detention or internal suspension - but this only works when the respect and trust are there.

In the next chapter, I will look again at pupil behaviour and share a more personal viewpoint, taking my own experience as my lodestar.

## Note

1 Paul Dix, *When the Adults Change, Everything Changes: Seismic Shifts in School Behaviour.* Pub Independent Thinking Press, 2017.

# 9 Behaviour – A personal view

Dealing with consistently poor behaviour is probably the most challenging aspect of Headship. The journey towards creating a culture of mutual respect and good behaviour begins for the Headteacher (and all the employees) with the simple question: *"Do you like children?"* For some, this might seem like a ludicrous question, as in *"Of course I like children. I wouldn't/couldn't possibly do the job if I didn't."* For others, this might well be a moment to reflect. I remember attending a Local Authority Heads Conference where the workshop leader asked us simply to take a moment to share with our paired colleagues what had brought us into education in the first place. I was a relatively new Head at the time, and my paired colleague quite the reverse. He had led a local boys' grammar school with an iron rod for many years and was proudly 'old school'. There was a long pause as he reflected on the question, and I was determined not to fill the silence for fear of saying something he might guffaw at. His answer didn't really surprise me, knowing his reputation. He said, "Well, it wasn't about the children, that's for sure."

I'm going to stick my neck out here by saying that you must, surely, like children to do this job. You must find talking to them, hearing their thoughts, interacting with them, and seeing them flourish something that makes you want to go into work every day. Having said that, I have never been remotely sentimental about this. I don't 'love the kids'; I don't find every little thing they do charming and delightful. They can be lazy, let you down, betray you, abuse you, and be a major source of stress. But at heart, I always have, on the whole, *enjoyed* being around the children in school. I am fascinated by their opinions about life, the universe, and school. I enjoy watching them emerge and develop as their cognitive powers mature. I get appropriately upset when things are going badly for them, and I am motivated by the creative challenge of finding better ways to make their time in school stimulating and enjoyable. As a Headteacher, I did get involved in the troubles experienced by individual pupils from time to time, but I was mostly concerned with designing and implementing systems and developing the skills of colleagues to ensure that, school-wide, things went well for more pupils every year.

These are the values that have underpinned the behaviour policies I adopted. The Headteacher has to *believe* in their policy; otherwise, it has no integrity or authenticity – and it will fail.

## Story from my first Headship

The story that follows reflects the values I brought to my first Headship, and an opportunity I had to translate those into a vision for the school after just a few days of being in post.

The school was in the East Midlands – a small setting in a cramped building. I took up the post in January, and before I arrived, I heard that the Year 10s had smashed all the baubles on the Christmas tree that was in the foyer of the gym. Not just one or two that had fallen foul as a result of some loutish jostling, but all of them, deliberately. I felt it was indicative of an attitude that was seriously awry. Conversations with teachers revealed that they were doing fine in the classroom but hanging on by their fingertips in the corridors and playground.

After I had been in post for around ten days, the foreman of the construction company working on a site adjacent to our playground came to see me in my office. He was polite and deferential, and asked if I would mind having a word with the kids in my school.

"Sure," I said. "What's the problem?"

"Well nothing much, really," he replied. "It's just that they keep lobbing stones over the fence and hitting my workers on the head."

Say what!?

I was left in no doubt at that point that the school I was now leading was in poor shape and I needed to do something. My previous experience had not prepared me for this, but I dug deep into my ten years' teaching experience and all the thinking I had done in qualifying and preparing for Headship. It seemed to me, as I consulted with my deputies, that we had a choice: we could tighten the rules to the point at which every child's feet were effectively nailed to the floor, or we could go the other way and loosen the regime I had inherited which was already rule-heavy and oppressive. Either way, I was going to make a radical change to the ethos of the school, and I was going to need to do so suddenly. Interestingly, I chose not to inform Governors or consult with staff because, frankly, I didn't yet know them well enough. This needed to be *my* decision and mine alone, and any guidance could only serve to water down my resolve and the authenticity of the announcement I planned to make.

I called an unscheduled assembly for the next morning. My speech went something like this:

> "As you know, I am new to this school and it has been a pleasure getting to know you all. I am glad I am here, and I have no regrets. However, recent events have caused me grave concern. The man in charge of the building site next door came to complain to me yesterday that pupils from this school were throwing rocks and stones over the fence on purpose, and these missiles were hitting his colleagues on the head and hurting them."

There was a bit of a gasp at that, and perhaps a snigger or two – I couldn't be sure, but the atmosphere suddenly became severe and hard. Utter breathless silence filled the hall as the community awaited my judgement. With my face set, I continued.

"So . . ." I looked down at my notes and sighed. I looked up and paused because my throat was tightening with emotion. "What we're going to do is . . . get rid of detention."

There was a beat and then a double take. Pupils who'd slumped in their seats, cowering at what they'd anticipated, suddenly sat up and turned to each other. "What did he just say?" I could hear them whisper. Some girls were laughing into the backs of their hands. The room murmured, and conversations gradually took hold. My face broke into a smile.

> "Well, let's face it, detention isn't working, is it? What we need is some trust, and I am going to trust you to get it right, every day, all day, and if you get it wrong, we'll talk about why, what went wrong, and what we can do to fix it in the future."

Understandably, that went down well with the pupils; this was a real change which positively affected their daily lives. However, some staff objected to this change. At the next staff meeting, the indignation burst like a boil.

"You have removed any leverage I had for instilling good behaviour in my lessons," intoned Steve, the chemistry teacher.

"Well, good-pace, well-planned lessons and a will to succeed should go a long way . . . ," I began.

"No, sorry, look . . . ." Alan, the Head of English, had interrupted me.

> "I'm sorry, Steve, but I am absolutely fed up with taking detention on a Friday afternoon, after school, and therefore effectively in my own time, to mop up the poor behaviour that has happened in *your* lessons. Not my lessons – yours. Why should I have to do that? Andrew is completely right. We need to deal with behaviour in our lessons ourselves and not simply pass the buck onto the system."

Steve was more grumpy than shocked, but Alan's intervention was pivotal. Behaviour improved dramatically overnight, and as a community we began a journey towards mutual respect being acted out in every interaction between its members, every day in every way.

It was a similar story in my second Headship. Some of the behaviour being exhibited by senior pupils (Year 11) was violent and brutish. Again, I applied a liberal and rational approach to behaviour management, but this time it was the parents who objected. Some of them complained about my leadership style nearly every day for about 15 months before finally settling down to a new way of working.

Then there was an incident on the playground which captured the tough journey I had been on personally as the new Headteacher. Five terms into second my Headship, I was on the playground and there was a huge commotion among some pupils in Years 7 and 8. They were all cheering and jeering, gathered in a circle around someone I couldn't see. I immediately assumed that there was a fight and strode forward through the crowd to break it up. When I got to the middle of the melee, I found a small 11-year-old boy demonstrating his break-dancing skills!

## Summary so far

My vision for a school with well-managed behaviour is to place a relentless emphasis on mutual respect between all the members of the community. It takes time, but the prize is a body of pupils who understand the benefits of self-regulation and how consistently respectful attitudes make school a more attractive proposition. There will always be outliers, but the policies that need to be applied to those pupils should not impinge on the honour shown to the majority who behave respectfully.

## 'Always explain and warn first'

I was surprised at the need to repeat and emphasise with staff the 'Always explain and warn first' rule. I had to explain that when I was picking up on a piece of behaviour that had been escalated to me, the pupil would often profess complete ignorance about what had got them into trouble: "All I did was drop my pencil and the teacher went crazy" was a common defence. I found it useful to give teachers a script, which went as follows:

> "Josh/Aadrika, I am giving you a warning now. What you're doing is [e.g., turning around and talking to the person behind you]. This behaviour is disrupting the learning of others in the class and so I need you to stop doing that and instead [important bit where you clearly describe the behaviour you want], I need you to sit at your desk, facing forward, and taking part in the lesson as directed by me. Do you understand what I am asking you to do?"

That might be a good example of a first warning. The second warning would have the same words but add a potential sanction at the end: "If you don't sit facing forward, I am going to have to ask you to leave the classroom. Do you understand?" All this is said with a calm professional tone of voice; it's witnessed by the whole class and so the child cannot claim later that he/she did not know what to do or that a sanction was delivered without clear instructions about how to avoid it. The tone of voice is very important, because it helps disguise any emotion you may have which does not belong in this situation. A calm tone of voice also gives the pupil the chance to justify their behaviour should they feel the need to and sometimes, of course, the pupil does have a reasonable explanation, and mutual respect is built by giving them the opportunity to explain.

I was surprised by the fact that I had to give this directive, because I thought it was obvious and that every teacher would do this. I was wrong, and although I risked coming across as condescending to some staff, it is always worth spelling out some of the basics, especially when new in post.

Behaviour policies come and go and details of what has happened in the past are lost. Some Headteachers, especially autocratic ones, can end up de-skilling their staff, leaving them unable to be appropriately autonomous in their interaction with pupils. In these circumstances, it can be necessary to re-educate and re-empower the teachers to trust their instincts and revert to relationships with pupils which are situated in the moment and are real.

## Behaviour and uniform rules

The level of compliance demanded around uniform rules is often controversial. There are many different interpretations across schools of how the uniform should be worn, and how tightly the rules should be enforced. Some Headteachers put uniform up front and centre and argue that *looking smart mirrors thinking smart* – or some such axiom. In other schools, pupils will interpret uniform rules very loosely indeed – to the point where all that remains is the white shirt, dark skirt or trousers and the tie, which is draped in various guises around the neck: the *St Trinian's*[1] look. Teachers in those schools treasure a sharp focus on the pupil in front of them, prioritising close, professional relationships over petty compliance with correct appearance.

When I arrived at my second Headship, I was aware that the community was not happy with the Uniform Policy and was looking to me to set the tone. I wanted to reach the ideal of "Pupils at this school look smart and wear the uniform with pride." Whilst endless corrections would be needed in the corridors, I also didn't want uniform to become a constant and ever-increasing bone of contention. So I decided that we would just take our time. If it took years – and several generations of pupils passing through the school – to arrive at my ideal, then so be it.

The policy didn't make me popular with either staff or pupils. Some staff felt I was being too soft and that improvements would never happen unless I licensed them to be tougher. Pupils felt perhaps a little betrayed that my raft of pupil-centred improvements was not matched by an easing of uniform restrictions. However, by being patient and also non-confrontational yet firm, the pupils ended up wanting to wear the uniform properly because it signalled their positive sense of belonging to the school community.

## Fairness

Perceived unfairness can generate poor behaviour across the whole school community. It is a priority for pupils, and it is easy to overlook. So concerned are we with safety, effective learning, and compliant behaviour that we don't see the elephant in the room, staring at us from the corner and making the pupils seriously angry. It is impossible for life in school to be entirely fair, but we should try our damnedest to make things as fair as possible. If any aspect of policy systematically leads to unfairness, is it any wonder the pupils respond badly? If adults are treated unfairly in the workplace, they get angry, go to human resources (HR), make a complaint, and ultimately end up in an employment tribunal if the unfairness is not corrected. Pupils have no such pathway; there is no HR department to appeal to. They just get angry, and that's all they have. (Except they can, of course, complain to their parents, and that leads to potential conflict – something that we'll look at in Part IV of this book.)

## Shaming

Paul Dix encourages us to accentuate the positive. Instead of writing the names of poorly behaved children on the board, which is just a form of public shaming, he recommends flipping it: make having your name on the board a *good* thing and something everyone in the room aspires to. The trouble with that idea is that you are still shaming the children who don't behave. The teacher is still seeking to encourage good behaviour – it's just that this time it is through the withholding of praise, but the effect is the same; it's still shaming. Shaming is horrible.

The shaming of pupils has no place in a well-run school. If you publicly shame and humiliate a pupil – for instance, making them stand up in an assembly because they are talking when they shouldn't be – that pupil may never forget or forgive you or the school for that moment. The pupil may not show their anger or try to explain what happened to their parents, partly because they were in the wrong in the first place, but if that pupil is influential amongst their peers, the school may well have sown the seeds for some troubled times ahead. The pupil may act out their resentment in any number of ways – disrupting, bullying, showing open disrespect, and deliberately under-achieving.

In this and the last chapter, I have looked at some of the most intractable dilemmas faced by schools around behaviour and how an ethos of mutual respect, built steadily and determinedly, can underpin the behaviour everyone desires.

I will end on the greatest conundrum of all, one which I suspect no school has ever successfully overcome: chewing gum.

## Chewing gum

For a while as Headteacher, I had the honour of teaching a nursery class on a weekly basis. I would bash away on the piano, singing *Old McDonald* to a group of fifteen 4-year-olds. They had zero respect for my status as Headteacher, and with all my teaching experience based in the secondary classroom, I had absolutely zero control over them. The nursery staff would stand on the other side of the classroom door vainly trying to stifle their laughter at my feeble attempts to conduct a proper lesson – something which came entirely naturally to them and at which they were highly skilled.

On one occasion I saw that one member of this nursery class – a boy – had something in his mouth, and I stopped to ask him what it was. He pulled out a piece of old chewing gum, and when I asked him where he had found it, he pointed at the dusty underside of a radiator. I used this story many times in assemblies as an illustration of why chewing gum was banned in the school. It made little difference: chewing gum at my school, like most, remained a persistent problem.

My response was therefore to escalate the rule about gum to the highest possible status; I couldn't bear it! My speech to the parents of new pupils emphasised how I tried to keep rules to a minimum, that the school's Behaviour Policy was based on community partnerships and respect. At the end of that speech I would conclude, "Except, of course, chewing gum. That is utterly banned, and I reserve my fiercest and most ugly ire for those caught with it." The line got a laugh, but I was being serious as well as ironic.

I suppose the point I'm making is that, despite all the co-created, harmonious, turbulence-free mission statements you apply to the school, there are moments of extreme exception:

> "DON'T CHEW GUM; IN FACT, DON'T BRING GUM INTO SCHOOL IN ANY FORM AT ANY TIME. IF I FIND GUM ON SOMEONE'S PERSON OR IN THEIR LOCKER, THERE WILL BE THE DIREST CONSEQUENCES IMAGINABLE. **HAVE I MADE MYSELF CLEAR?**"

For all that bluster, the effect was marginal.

## Note

1  St Trinian's, *Ealing Studios*. Produced and Directed by Parker and Thompson, 2007.

# 10 Bullying

Bullying is an ugly side of human nature – a by-product of an imbalance of power within relationships. It happens in the workplace, in the home, and it happens in school. No matter how harmonious, mutually supportive, and respectful the relational cultures in the school are, bullying still happens.

It tends to happen far less often than some parents would have the school believe – the curse of crying "Wolf!" is a real and present problem. It also probably happens a bit *more* often than pupils are prepared to admit to adults – the curse of 'snitching' is also a real and present problem.

## Some parents over-react

The problem of parents crying "Wolf!" over bullying stems from statutory guidance that all accusations of bullying must be addressed promptly to safeguard and protect the wellbeing of children. Some parents, whose children complain of even the slightest conflict with peers, feel justified in requiring the school to investigate bullying. Anecdotally, teachers often tell me that very few claims of bullying are actually substantiated, even after lengthy investigation. Spurious – and even vexatious – claims of bullying clog up the system and often make things worse for pupils.

Therefore, when creating an anti-bullying policy, it is important to include the definition. According to KCSiE: bullying is generally defined as the following:

**Repeated** behaviour, rather than one-off incidents.
**Intentional** harm-doing, where the perpetrator or perpetrators aim to cause distress or harm.
**Imbalance of power**, where the person or people being bullied have difficulty defending themselves due to the power held by the perpetrator(s). This power could be, for example: physical strength, access to embarrassing information, or popularity.

Bullying can take various forms, including the following:

**Physical bullying**: Hitting, kicking, pushing, or any other form of physical aggression.
**Verbal bullying**: Name-calling, insults, teasing, intimidation, or verbal abuse.
**Emotional bullying**: Spreading rumours, excluding someone from a group, or other actions intended to harm someone's social relationships.
**Cyberbullying**: Bullying using electronic means such as social media, text messages, emails, or other online platforms.

It is important to have the definition clear, and perhaps even copied into the home school agreement because it can often be misinterpreted by parents.

A short paragraph in the anti-bullying policy pointing out the dangers of interpreting peer-to-peer **conflict** as bullying is useful. The school will take reports of conflict between pupils equally seriously as it does accusations of bullying, but making a distinction between the two is vital.

## Many to one; one to many

In my experience, the moment bullying is revealed is always a shock. When a couple of boys quietly admitted they were really uncomfortable with the way 40 other boys were teasing their friend under the guise of 'banter', it rocked the staff room, because no one could quite believe this was happening. The time some Year 7s asked the teacher if it was okay to be giving £1 coins to a boy in Year 9 because he pleaded with them, but with menace, we all thought, "How could this happen?" But it does, and it is not necessarily a failure of leadership or systems.

## Bullying between girls

Deciding whether or not bullying is happening is complex. Jessica Ringrose[1] argues that when it comes to girls specifically, the anti-bullying policy is a blunt tool and is over-applied. She writes,

> What is troubling is [that] a school psychology literature is now amassing that takes girls' indirect and/or relational aggression as a premise for behavioural management and anti-bully policy.
> 
> (p. 411)

In other words, when girls fall out, they can indeed be mean to each other and sometimes the balance of power can become lopsided. That doesn't make it bullying, and the *Girls on Board* approach is precisely the tool needed by schools, as she points to in her conclusion:

> It would seem new conceptual frameworks for approaching girls' conflict are needed that critically engage with the limitations of the psychological discourses of aggression and bullying.
> 
> (p. 415)

Between girls, in my experience, bullying is rare. Conflict, when it arises, can very often be summed up by the useful phrase *'normal-if-regrettable friendship turbulence'*. The solution is the evocation of empathy, using guided reflection – not investigation and sanctions.

Even if an investigation concludes that bullying has taken place, we have to question whether the sanctions prescribed by the anti-bullying policy are the best way to resolve the situation and restore harmony. Take a girl in Year 12 who has been ostracised by all the other girls in her year group because she is going out with a boy who used to date her (now ex-)best friend. For the whole of her 6th form experience, she has no female companionship and must rely on her own resilience to fill that void. Most teachers would regard that as a clear example of *many-to-one* bullying, but what is the school going to do about it? The Head of Year telling off every girl in Year 12 is not going to make things better for the victim. Sanctions need to fit the situation, not the crime, and focus must always remain on trying to achieve the best outcomes for all concerned.

## Bullying between boys and the problem of banter

Banter is the exchange of teasing remarks designed to deliver a mild and amusing moment of humiliation. But it can go too far and that is often the source of bullying between boys. Attempts to control or even ban banter are rarely effective because this form of communication is *natural* for boys – and some girls too. Banter is a form of verbal jousting akin to lion cubs play-fighting, and too much adult intervention feels intrusive and alienating. As I argue in *Working with Boys*, the best way to guide boys in their banter is to promote self-regulation and that is achieved through lessons using guided reflection. Boys of all ages *know* that the banter can go too far and become hurtful. They also *know* that sexualised banter is wrong and is used for cheap laughs to gain social influence. Holding up a non-judgemental mirror to this form of behaviour – repeatedly – brings about self-correction and peer-agreed mutual respect.

## National campaigns – do they work?

I have never been a fan of national anti-bullying campaigns. Their aims are to raise awareness of bullying, encouraging victims to speak up and bystanders to call it out.

The strategies these campaigns use seem questionable to me. Some schools train pupils to be anti-bullying ambassadors – the idea is that they act as upstanding models of good relational behaviour and are unafraid to challenge bullying where they witness it. Their pictures are posted in the corridors and classrooms, and they are introduced to the pupils in assemblies. Pupils are also encouraged to seek the help and support of an ambassador if they feel the need.

I operated a similar scheme in my school for a while; a small group of senior pupil volunteers were trained up to be 'peer mentors'. The training was interesting, and I think those pupils gained some insight into how to be supportive and helpful to younger peers. But in reality, no one ever sought help from these mentors – not even once.

I also had real doubts about the selection process for the Anti-Bullying Ambassador training, and I know for sure that one boy who was selected was himself a bully. Perhaps I should have stepped in, but that would have involved making uncomfortable accusations for which I had insufficient evidence. Some schools may have experienced positive outcomes from having Ambassadors, but it feels counter-intuitive to me. It feels like the Ambassadors carry too much responsibility and would be accused of snitching and/or interfering if they got involved in the dynamics of friendships and interactions between pupils outside their immediate sphere.

I also doubt the effectiveness of Anti-Bullying Week. In a literature review undertaken by the Anti-Bullying Alliance in 2019, only two strategies were deemed as 'strong' in tackling bullying:

**Improve school climate:** Pupils need to feel safe and happy in school. Promote high-quality pupil–pupil relationships and high-quality teacher–pupil relationships.
**Authoritative school climate:** Promote high disciplinary and academic expectations for students. Teachers and other school staff members interact with students in a respectful, caring, and helpful manner.

In both strategies, the emphasis is on mutual respect between peers and between staff and pupils. If having a series of assemblies, posters on the wall, role-plays, and storytelling helps improve the quality of inter-personal relationships in the school, then Anti-Bullying Week is effective. We just have to ask how this can be sustained throughout the school year.

The best anti-bullying strategy would therefore seem to be to focus on improving these relationships through the central tenets being promoted in this book:

- The aggregation of marginal gains to the daily experiences of pupils.
- Making school an attractive place where pupils feel safe and would rather attend than not attend.

## Watch and listen

Bullying by its nature is often hidden. It happens online, in the lavatories, on the way to and from school. Therefore, the most effective thing staff can do is watch and listen. Never be complacent, and look out for all the clues and indicators we learn about in our safeguarding training. After that idea has been acknowledged and absorbed by staff, there need to be easy and accessible ways to share information. We need staff to keep the threshold of reporting low, but we also need to *talk*. Short, frequent meetings – perhaps 15 minutes before school starts – in which pupils of concern are discussed is a very powerful mechanism and one that is sadly overlooked in favour of exclusive online reporting.

## Who is included in the policy?

In Part IV of this book, we will look at the role parents can play in helping to run a school successfully. Before we get there, and as we conclude this chapter on bullying, we need to consider the relationship between parents and the anti-bullying policy. Are parents mentioned, and if not, why not? Parents are not entitled to behave aggressively to any member of staff. Persistent recurrence of such behaviour needs to be labelled for what it is: bullying. Staff, as much as any member of the school community, need protection from bullies, and the anti-bullying policy needs to be crystal clear on that.

## Summary

Bullying will always occur in schools, and the aim must always be to keep it to a minimum and never be complacent. The best strategies are focused on mutually respectful relational cultures.

## Note

1 Jessica Ringrose, 'Just be friends': Exposing the limits of educational bully discourses for understanding teen girls' heterosexualized friendships and conflicts. *British Journal of Sociology in Education*, 29(5), 509–522, 2008.

# 11 Policy writing

Policy writing can feel like a chore. It *is* a chore – but an important one, and one which isn't without its creative and self-expressive elements.

Much of what a Headteacher is and does is reflected in school policy, and those policies are either written – or at least approved – by the Head. This chapter is included in Part II – Children, because policies should always be written with the child in mind.

The sheer volume of required policies has ballooned in recent decades, and that has added considerably to the administrative burden on the Headteacher. I laughed out loud when I read that I needed a 'policy on policies', but actually it was quite liberating. Far from being tokenistic, the Policy on Policies gave me the chance to express my view that policies need to be the following:

- pithy
- as brief as possible
- generic rather than specific (usually)
- written in plain English

## Audience

Policies consolidate and enshrine the vision and values of the school. In choosing language and style for the policy, the Headteacher needs to bear in mind the audience.

1. Initially, the policy is likely to be read and closely scrutinised by the Governing Body, or Top Layer. It is easy, with a Governing Body meeting coming up, to write the policy with this in mind, but the audience is much wider. Schools where the Top Layer is a Multi-Academy Trust (MAT), or proprietor group, may receive policies from above; some may come from the Local Authority. That will save time, but the Headteacher would be wise to challenge the wording if it does not fit their setting. Similarly, using artificial intelligence (AI) can be helpful, but every sentence needs to be checked for accuracy.
2. The policy will be read by **parents**, often when they are unhappy. Parents pursuing a grievance against the school will – quite rightly – seek clarification from the bank of policies about the validity of their potential complaint. That's why ensuring that the policies are about the pupils is important. For example, a policy that restricts staff from leaving the premises without Senior Leadership Team (SLT) permission is about ensuring there are always enough staff on site to keep pupils safe.
3. The policies – a great many of which must, by law, be published on the school's website – may be read by **journalists** seeking a story after an incident. Policies therefore need to be formal and neutral, leaving no room for misinterpretation.
4. Finally, **lawyers** – often commissioned by a complaining parent – will look at policies to find the slightest gap they can manipulate to justify their case against the school. It might, therefore, be tempting to have a lawyer look over all policies as a way of mitigating

this risk but, in my experience, this is not money well spent. First, the inspectorate bodies have no respect for the fact that a policy has been written and/or approved by a law firm; they alone will judge whether a policy is compliant. Second, lawyers rarely offer *guarantees* that their authorship or approval will pre-empt or prevent litigation. They therefore have no 'skin in the game'. Headteachers are just as well educated as most lawyers but have thought longer and harder about how to run a school and should therefore trust themselves.

## Universality

Although policies are supposed to cover any and every eventuality, there will probably always be holes in the attempt to be comprehensive. A Headteacher can therefore expect to be writing new policies or updating existing ones, with perhaps surprising regularity. This is best practice and allows the school to learn from things as they happen.

For example, let's say some staff start creating social media groups for informal sharing out of school. Some remarks posted are unprofessional and are seen by a parent. The policy on staff conduct needs to be updated to include specifically the use of closed social media groups (not just posting on open forums) and the absolute need for professionalism in both working and non-working hours.

Another example: pupils start coming to school on e-scooters, creating the need for a possible new policy dealing with transport to and from school. This policy might then consolidate previously unrecorded rules about the wearing of uniform and behaviour on public transport and useful support mechanisms for pupils if they feel or become unsafe at the beginning and end of the day.

## Summary

The suite of school policies will never be complete and should be regarded as ongoing and reviewable.

# 12 Finding balance and working with children

In Chapter 3 on finding balance, I suggested some generic principles to follow. In this chapter, to conclude Part II on children, I will look at the stresses and strains that are particularly associated with the responsibility of looking after and educating children.

I am an admirer of Dr Jill Berry's book *Making the Leap*,[1] and much of my thinking in this chapter is influenced by her book and my long professional association with her.

Let's suppose *you* are the new Headteacher – the new boss.

As a new Headteacher, the way you deal with difficulty largely defines you. In challenging circumstances, the community will observe not just the decisions you make and strategies you deploy but how the situation is affecting you personally as well. Do you remain calm, controlled, and in command of the situation, or does a degree of emotional vulnerability creep in which might undermine people's confidence in your inner strength? On the other hand, perhaps that little display of vulnerability isn't actually a bad thing. It can be a powerful way to show that tough moments *do* affect you – that you are human and alive to the pressures facing everyone in these moments. The balance to be struck is between showing the strength that people need to rely on and being demonstrably vulnerable enough to be empathetic with other people's emotional turmoil.

For example, if you have to announce to staff the untimely death of a recently retired colleague, there needs to be a moment of shared grief, but you cannot afford to be overwhelmed by that. After the moment of reflection, the community will need you to lead from the front again, showing acuity and judgement in the selection of events that will commemorate the lost colleague. This may seem obvious, but once in post, this level of analysis is a significant part of projecting to the community who you are and what you stand for. The self-examination in itself may feel like you are cynically objectifying and controlling your personal response, but that's the job – perhaps the biggest difference between being the Headteacher and any other role in the school.

Dr Berry quotes Robert Quinn's[2] idea that the new Headteacher has to "build the bridge as they walk on it". No amount of preparation will actually establish how the community will view your effectiveness as Head; that can only be done in post and, sadly, is usually judged by your response to challenge in its many forms. And of course, no matter how many years' experience you have had as a senior deputy and teacher, you will never have faced these challenges *as a Headteacher* before – you are learning on the job.

You will likely surprise yourself at how well you cope with the stresses and emotional strain of challenging moments. On the other hand, you may find yourself emotionally upended when you least expect it. But you learn from that, and you make sure you have enough supporters to get you through. Those supporters may come from home and/or friends outside the school, or they may come from within the staff and/or Governors – trusted colleagues. Becoming part of professional networks is also a very effective way of finding support and calibrating your emotional responses to events.

## Who's the boss?

You are no longer working to please the boss because you *are* the boss. You learn, instead, to *love* the school, set your *own* targets. But at the same time, you remain objective and relentlessly professional. It's a job – a job you can choose to walk away from at any time, but also a job which, to be done well, needs your full personal commitment. In order not to be overwhelmed, you also have to realise you *aren't* actually the school, merely its guardian and keeper until the next person takes over from you.

## Death of a child

All of this may go some way to preparing you for the most awful and tragic moment: the death of a child. When it happened to me, I found myself having to rely on an inner dialogue to ensure that my response was appropriate to my role rather than my personal feelings. I knew that I had an important job directly after the funeral: I needed to find the dead child's twin brother and offer some words of comfort and reassurance. If I had been unable to do that, I would have been letting everyone down.

There is no moment when you're not the Head, yet there is enormous pride to be had in acknowledging and embodying that. The job comes with enormous challenges and enormous rewards: knowing that you have led a community through its darkest hours and helped everyone, collectively and individually, find the light at the end of the tunnel is a unique privilege.

## Notes

1 Jill Berry, *Making the Leap*. Pub Crown House Publishing, 2016.
2 Robert Quinn, *Building the Bridge as You Walk on it: A Guide for Leading Change*. Pub Jossey-Bass, p. 137, 2011.

# Part III: Staff

# 13 Being a unique employer

Let's start with **McGregor's X-Y Theory of Management**, which helps leaders understand how their beliefs about employees can influence their management style.

The theory proposes two contrasting views of human nature and motivation in the workplace.

## Theory X

**Assumptions:** This theory assumes that employees are inherently lazy, dislike work, and will avoid responsibility. Therefore, they need to be closely supervised and controlled to achieve organisational goals.

**Management style:** Managers who adopt these assumptions often micromanage, using authoritarian methods, relying on strict rules, and imposing penalties for non-compliance.

## Theory Y

**Assumptions:** In contrast, Theory Y assumes that employees are self-motivated, enjoy their work, and seek responsibility. This theory suggests that, when led in the right way, employees will take initiative and contribute creatively to the school.

**Management style:** Managers who embrace the assumptions of Theory Y typically foster a more supportive environment, encouraging collaboration and autonomy.

In essence, McGregor's theories highlight how a manager's beliefs about human nature can significantly impact their approach to management. While Theory X might lead to a more controlled workplace, Theory Y fosters an environment of trust and self-motivation, ultimately leading to higher employee satisfaction and productivity.

By managing *all* employees with the assumption that they are self-motivated professionals, keen to do the best job they can, the Headteacher will increase the number of employees who perform that way. You remove the excuse that some employees fall back on, which is to blame their laziness on lack of management trust and meaningful delegation. You will also create a self-improving, high-performing workforce who appreciate you and love their jobs. You can maintain the workforce's excellence through simple acts of gratitude, acknowledgement, and validation.

If an employee fails to respond to Theory Y management by improving their performance and attitude, you can begin the process of terminating their contract safe in the knowledge that any claim to an employment tribunal for constructive wrongful dismissal is likely to fail.

In other words, using the Theory Y management orientation is not soft or conflict-avoidant; it does not mean the Headteacher is failing to hold employees to account.

## Is this a good place to work?

Any employer would surely want the answer to "Is this a good place to work?" to be a resounding "Yes!". However, it can be a bit more nuanced than that.

In a school, the Headteacher doesn't want the "Yes" to be because of the following:

- "The boss doesn't really care what I do and never checks up on me, so the job is a doss."
- "We're usually overstaffed, so I don't have that much to do."
- "I'd leave, but the pay here is crazy high, so there's no point."
- "The boss is a push-over and caves into any demand we make."

The Headteacher hopes it's a good place to work because of the following:

- "The work is stimulating and challenging enough to keep me on my toes."
- "The school shows its gratitude for my hard work through words of affirmation to me personally and my colleagues collectively."
- "The school shows its appreciation of my work by being reasonably generous: free tea, coffee, and biscuits and lunch. The pay is competitive."
- "Where possible, the school always acknowledges the pressures of my life outside of work. The school is generous in granting me permission to take special time off if it's justified – like my toddler's Nativity or my parents' golden wedding anniversary."
- "The school notices if I go the extra mile; they may not be able to pay overtime, but at least the work I do is acknowledged and I am thanked."
- "The school is always keen to explore ways to facilitate my work so that I can perform more effectively and contribute to a well-run school."
- "The school listens to my ideas for innovation and tries to incorporate those ideas if it can."
- "The school facilitates my personal and professional growth through allowing me time and giving me funding to train, read and study."
- "The school will always have my back and support me if conflict with pupils or parents arises. If I am in the right, they will always reassure me of my professionalism. If I am in the wrong, they will support me and help me correct, learn, and recover without being unduly humiliated or traumatised."
- "The leaders of the school are always calm. They don't shout or get visibly angry. Their presence is reassuring and sets a tone in which every employee can feel safe, appreciated and can thrive."

The Headteacher should be able to recognise all the positives in these examples, and if they can't (looking at this from the employee's point of view), then it probably isn't a great place to work. If it isn't a great place to work and it's hard to recruit and retain staff as a result, then what justification does the Head give for that? I don't think 'lack of money' is an excuse, because what price are you putting on a happy staff and ensuring there is a high-quality, well-trained teacher in every classroom? What price for staff morale? What price for innovators being given free rein? What price for every employee telling everyone they know, *"This is a good place to work"*?

So why does this make the Headteacher a unique employer? Because each reason quoted in these examples will have been delivered by a unique individual in a unique way.

# 14 Leadership style

## From day-to-day to strategic

An experienced colleague once described to me the first few years of his Headship. At first, he involved himself closely in all the detail and staff came to see him to present problems and ask for solutions. After a while, staff learned to present possible solutions for themselves and asked only for his steer. After a further while, his role was to listen and approve while staff described the solutions they were putting in place. Eventually, the work being done to run the school from day to day was reported to him at weekly update meetings with senior leaders. Over the course of a few terms, his staff had gained a deep understanding of his vision for the school and the values that underpinned that vision. Staff were able to anticipate what decisions he was likely to make, and he trusted them to act without his constant sign-off. In other words, he was delegating, and that allowed him to be more strategic. I suggest this is an excellent model. If the Headteacher can't stop micromanaging the organisation after a suitable amount of time, for whatever reason, then the school has problems!

## What is 'strategic'?

Although the question, 'What does the Head do all day long?' can solicit some amusing answers (e.g. "I care"), it can be a genuine mystery to the community. However, here's what being **strategic** - having a focus on the long term and overall aims of the school - includes the following:

- Reviewing performance indicators such as numbers on roll; academic assessment data; predicted grades in public exams; results in public exams; rates of sanctions by gender, year group, etc.; rates of complaints; staff sickness and tardiness; projects on the School Development Plan (SDP).
- Working with the Top Layer (Governors, MAT leaders, proprietors, etc.) preparing reports for the main Board meetings and sub-committees such as Finance, Grounds and Buildings, Personnel, and Academic.
- Working on finance: preparing and monitoring budgets, writing grant proposals.
- Parent satisfaction surveys.
- Staffing analysis and deployment of human resources.
- Pupil Voice surveys.
- Site development, planning, working with architects, builders, and the Local Authority.
- Working with neighbours and local institutions.
- Preparing for inspection and overseeing compliance.
- Reviewing and writing policies.

## Day-to-day

While we are listing 'things Heads do', it's useful to look at tasks that are more regular and not particularly strategic, i.e. the Headteacher's ongoing contribution to the day-to-day running of the school:

- Reading and writing reports for pupils
- Learning walks
- Appraisals
- Meetings with line managers within the academic and support/administration structures of the school
- Meeting prospective parents
- Interviewing candidates for new staff positions
- Communicating with staff, parents, outside agencies, and the Top Layer
- Dealing with behaviour
- Teaching, marking, and lesson preparation
- Working with senior leaders
- Working with information technology (IT) staff and the network manager
- Touring the site
- Teaching

## Spare capacity

Headship is a busy job, but the Head should be careful not to appear permanently too busy. A Headteacher who gives the impression that they are constantly hanging on by their fingertips does not inspire confidence and is not a good role model for work/life balance, either. Heads need to stay on top of the workload, and if things are regularly overwhelming, they need to undertake a serious review of workflow.

It is the Headteacher's *job* to remain calm and in control. That means it is the Head's *job* to go home and relax in good time in order to be fresh and fully energised the next day. It also means having spare capacity so that the diary and plans for the working day can be put on hold for a while, not just to allow for reflection time but also to be able to react when only the Headteacher's input will do.

Here are some examples of why spare capacity is critical.

The Deputy Head rings. "A Year 9 boy has brought alcohol into school. I have taken written statements from pupils who witnessed it, and it's down to you to talk to him and decide on next steps."

The Office rings. "Josh, in Year 4? His father was taken to hospital and is very unwell. Can you call Josh's mum back now please, because she won't be available after she leaves the house in ten minutes."

A girl in Year 10 knocks on your door. "I need to tell you something very serious, and I need your help . . ."

These are the sorts of things that happen weekly in any school community, and if the Headteacher has no spare capacity to engage rapidly, or even immediately where needed, then these 'live and ongoing' situations will get worse. Not only will they get worse, but people in the community will also start to question the Head's sense of priorities and, therefore, their reputation.

There will be pinch points in the year when the workload is high; it can be useful to say that to the staff:

> "The next few days are going to be exceptionally busy for me as I [finalise preparation for inspection/finish our review of compliance/interview for new posts etc.], so I may not

be quite as available as I would like to be. If it's urgent, of course I will always make time for you."

## Mucking in

Every school leader needs to decide whether they're prepared to muck in or not. Let's say it's the school play and the curtain is about to drop for the interval. Someone tells you the loos are blocked, and the site staff are not returning until the end of the evening to lock up. As Headteacher, would you muck in? Either way, this dilemma says a lot about your leadership style.

## How visible is the Head?

I recall a girl who joined my school mid-year from a local school with more than 2,000 pupils. She told me that about three days before she left that school, having been there through Year 7 and half of Year 8, she saw a woman in the corridor she didn't recognise.

"Who's that?" she asked her friend.

"That's the Headteacher" was the reply.

When a Headteacher takes up a new post, the decision about how visible they will be needs to be decided on day one. Nothing quite captures your attitude towards being present, visible, hands-on, and there to help more than your choice to have an 'open door' policy. 'Open door' does not mean it is always open, because the Headteacher will need to have meetings which are private. But when deskwork is all that is being done, having the door open encourages fluent and efficient communication, and good communication is the oil that keeps the whole machinery of school life running smoothly. There might be nervousness about this policy inviting too many people to come to the door or about feeling bounced into hasty decisions by a delegation that stretches down the corridor. If that is the case, the door can always be closed for a while to give some breathing space.

I do recommend an open door; my school wasn't very big, and so it was perhaps easier to cope than if it were bigger; nonetheless, the number of quick conversations I had was huge. No need to put themselves in the diary and wait for the next appointment – children and staff could just pop in to ask a question, pose an idea, or update me on a recent conversation. From both their point of view and mine, it was 'job done'; let's move on to the next thing.

Head thinks: "It's 10:15am and I fancy my morning coffee right now. No, I'll leave it until 10:30am, then I can have it in the staff room with my employees." Time in the staff room, even just reading the trade papers for ten minutes, is never wasted time.

## Time out of school

As time passes and the Headteacher becomes appropriately more and more strategic in their thinking and actions, opportunities to spend time out of school may arise. The Head may choose to inspect other schools or attend regular sector or local meetings. These outside interests are entirely appropriate because they feed into the overall experience and wisdom of the Headteacher. It is often from these outside interests that new ideas are brought back to school to become part of new drivers for improvement. The Headteacher who *never* leaves the school risks becoming insular, blinkered, and, ultimately, out of date.

# 15 Leadership competencies

Much is made of the *qualities* needed to be a good school leader – soft skills, emotional intelligence, intellectual capacity, strong vision and values, charisma, a commanding presence. Hidden behind these grand and noble attributes are the more mundane but equally important **competencies**. Being well organised and tech savvy defines how *efficient* a Headteacher is, and if they are not efficient, then being led by them is frustrating and limiting.

## Email

The way people use emails varies considerably across all sectors of society, whether in leadership roles or not. Email has significantly increased the volume of communication coming into schools. The Headteacher can expect dozens of emails a day which need a response. Here is a set of questions which will guide reflection on attitudes to email.

1. If it is a straightforward email, do you reply now or leave it to later? If you leave it to later, how do you ensure you don't miss it? Do you mark it as 'unread', or drag and drop it to a special 'to do folder' or some other folder?
2. If it is an email that is going to need a considered reply, how do you make time for that? Do you set aside time in your diary, make time at the end of the day, take it home, or let it sit there in your inbox for a while and see what happens?
3. Do you regard the speed of your replies to be a significant indicator of your efficiency? Does it irritate you when other people take longer to reply than you do?
4. Do you let your Personal Assistant (PA) handle your inbox? If so, how do you deal with confidential emails?
5. Have you discovered the time-saving trick of using 'text replacement' short cuts? For example, you can type the email greeting used in early January every year by using just three key strikes. So, "Dear, Happy New Year and I trust you had a good break over the Christmas holidays." is generated automatically by just typing something like 'dea'. The time saved each time you use this 'hack' is small but quickly adds up. (Google this if it doesn't make sense.)
6. Do you set aside a specific, diarised time in the day to deal with emails, or is it more organic – grabbing time when it arises?
7. What is your attitude to sending or responding to emails outside school hours? Do you never do this or perhaps only to other senior colleagues – or is it fine to engage with parents out of hours, too?
8. Do you have your work emails on your phone? If so, are you tempted to check them in the evenings and weekends? Does that actually save you time, or is it an unnecessary source of stress preventing you from unwinding?

## Know your management of information system (MIS)

The school's MIS is one of the most expensive subscription items in the IT or administrative budget. It is often capable of a lot more than is realised by many schools. The Headteacher can set a good example by being one of the better users of the system, knowing how to navigate it, mining its data, and showing others how to get the best from it, too. The excuse of having a teaching background in Literature and/or the Arts doesn't wash anymore!

## Use a digital diary

Use a digital diary and use it well. When the Headteacher is asked in the corridor if there is space in the diary for a quick chat today, the diary should be readily accessible on a mobile device there and then. Anything less than that – such as, "Please check with my PA" – is inefficient.

## The competencies needed to manage people – "You're fired!"

There are lots of euphemisms for terminating an employee's contract, including the following:

- sacked
- fired
- let go
- dismissed
- managed out

This is undoubtedly a tricky aspect of running a school, and so here's a checklist.

1. Contact your HR adviser.

That's it. That's the checklist – and I cannot emphasise enough how *anything* that a Headteacher does without HR guidance is likely to end up going wrong for them and the school.

## Protected conversations

There is a useful part of employment law which allows the employer to have a 'protected conversation' with an employee. That means the employer can have a frank discussion with the employee without prejudice. This is a useful mechanism to encourage, perhaps, an employee to reflect on the path they are currently taking in relation to their employment and change direction before they come into direct conflict with the school. An employer may not have a 'protected conversation' without setting it up properly first. The set-up cannot be done retrospectively, nor can anything be said that might be deemed discriminatory against the protected characteristics as defined in the Equality Act 2010. The employee has to agree to it, and it is explained that anything that is said cannot be used as grounds for wrongful dismissal.

## Settlement agreements

Sadly, employees who have had their contract terminated often make a claim for compensation on the basis of some form of unfairness or discrimination. However certain the employer may be that dismissal was entirely justified and the process handled with expert advice every step of the way, counter claims from the employee will inevitably take up time and energy. It is often therefore expedient to make a financial offer to the employee in the form of a settlement agreement. Within reason, the financial sum can be paid tax free, but a non-disclosure agreement (NDA) is the quid pro quo. The NDA prevents both sides from sharing any information about the circumstances of the departure of the staff member or what led up to it. The NDA will probably need to contain the text of an agreed reference to be used by the employee for finding new employment.

After negotiation, and before the settlement agreement is confirmed, two weeks must elapse and the employer must fund legal advice for the employee, which must be taken. A lawyer once advised me that if both parties feel slightly aggrieved at the end of an employment dispute, that is probably the best outcome!

## General Data Protection Regulations (GDPR)

From the moment concerns are raised about an employee's performance, with dismissal as a possible outcome, it is important to stop using the employee's name or even initials in written records. Written records include minutes of meetings and email exchanges, and any formal or informal messaging. Under GDPR, an employee may make a subject access request (SAR) at any point – meaning that they are entitled to see all documentation held by the school which makes any clear reference to that person. Redactions can be made in that documentation in order to protect the privacy of others. In corresponding with senior colleagues, HR, and people in the Top Layer about this employee, a pseudonym therefore needs to be adopted which can be agreed upon verbally. There is nothing to stop managers from altering mentions of the employee's name retrospectively – as long as that is done *prior* to a SAR being lodged.

## Minimum professional standards

There are many lamentable forms of employee behaviour that might invoke the 'gross misconduct' clause in the employment contract. How that is dealt with should always be subject to immediate advice from HR.

If, however, an employee has been underperforming and it is time to put them 'on competencies', then here are some tips. Putting an employee 'on competencies' simply means laying out the areas of 'minimum professional standards' that are not currently being met. (The expression 'minimum professional standards' is better, I think, than 'on competencies'.) For example, a teacher is failing to mark homework on time, and the quality of the marking and written feedback does not meet standards laid down in the school's Marking and Assessment Policy. A meeting is held with the teacher, with a third-party present – e.g. a Deputy Head – for triangulation. The minimum standards the teacher is failing to meet are laid out clearly and carefully. The teacher's opinion is sought and acknowledged. Targets are set with clear deadlines, and the next meeting is diarised then and there. Minutes are produced and the teacher is given the right to suggest alterations. After that, HR will guide the next steps. HR tend to advise face-to-face meetings, as opposed to email exchanges, because they strengthen the process if it is challenged at employment tribunal.

## Aftermath

The need to dismiss employees is almost inevitable at some point, so it is important to brace yourself emotionally. If the employee fails to get another post in teaching – something they love – then they needed to be better at their job. It's not your fault!

# 16 Technology in school

Technology has revolutionised education several times in the last 30 years. With each wave of technological innovation, teachers have had to re-evaluate not only their pedagogical style but even their very purpose. Remember the debate about Google replacing teachers? More recently, the existential question has become, "How do we structure independent learning tasks designed to introduce new learning and consolidate existing knowledge that can't just be done by the pupil using AI?" Even if Google didn't change much for teachers, AI will certainly force them to think hard about how we retain the usefulness of homework, projects, essay writing, and research.

All teachers must embrace the use of technology, whether that's in communicating through email, using online platforms for report writing, or recording assessments on the school's MIS. Not every teacher is comfortable with high levels of engagement with technology, and it is important to remain open to the possibility that the use of technology does not always make people more efficient or their communications clearer. The Headteacher can't come across as a Luddite without damaging their credibility to some extent, whereas keeping on top of technological advances can create a strong impression of competence and modernity. But technology is expensive, and investing in the latest innovation does not always lead to improvements in teaching and learning, or pupil engagement.

## WOW – Write in the Wall

Sometimes, low-tech solutions can more effective than the latest gizmo. For instance, interactive whiteboards are not always necessary in every classroom, whereas it is always useful to be able to jot something on an 'analogue' whiteboard. It can be a great idea to turn the whole classroom into one big old-style whiteboard. By smoothing the plasterwork and applying specialist whiteboard paint, pupils can access the walls as if they were a canvas. Their workings, poems, and collaborative work can be seen by all, and they can do this work standing up. The uses for this simple innovation are almost endless and, after I introduced it at my school, I never tired of enthusing about it to prospective parents; it is simply a great idea. The pupils also liked the WOW walls and their introduction was a good example of a small improvement in their daily experience of school.

## Investing in IT

Before purchasing new software or devices, here is a checklist to go through:

1. Perform an audit of how this new technology will improve teaching and learning. Will it make learning easier and more effective? Will it save teachers' time and effort?
2. Consider how the new technology will be received by pupils. Will they regard it as an additional chore, or will they be motivated by it, raising their levels of engagement?

3. Consider how the new technology will be received by parents. If the new technology relates to communication, will it make things simpler? There have been many changes in the platforms used to communicate with parents over the years – will this latest change be seen as just another fad?
4. Consider how the new technology will be received by teachers. Is this good for some subject areas or age groups but not for others? Is this a tool which will make life easier for senior leaders but is a chore for teachers and support staff?

The successful implementation of all these ideas is dependent on carefully designed **induction**, which will need to be differentiated for pupils, parents, and staff. The time and human resources needed to introduce and embed new technology is often underestimated. I remember introducing a Year 7 cohort to the idea that they had individual accounts on the school network. We asked them to create a password and then, no more than two minutes later, asked them to sign in with the name and the password they had just created. In those two minutes, about a third of them had forgotten their password, and the whole process took twice as long as predicted! When introducing a major new teaching and learning platform, I gave every teacher one period a week to learn how to use the new software – admittedly, we were slightly overstaffed that year – but it meant there could be no excuses about 100% uptake being required

## Managing IT

When you include the wages of the manager and support staff, IT is a huge budget item – and it needs to be managed well. A weekly meeting with the Network Manager (or equivalent) attended by Deputy Head Curriculum, Headteacher, and Business Manager is probably appropriate. The inclusion of the business manager is not always necessary but can be useful if they have a good feel and enthusiasm for uses of IT. Their presence might be to represent non-teaching staff rather than advise on affordability, since a budget will already have been set.

There are always things to say, decisions to make, and plans to anticipate and monitor. A school that is on top of its use of IT will give the impression of competence and be regarded by the most insouciant of pupils as at least 'all right'. Whilst not necessarily having to be an expert, a Headteacher who is thoroughly knowledgeable about technology will keep the IT staff on their toes and encourage them in a job which can otherwise feel rather remote.

## The internet on pupils' desks

We know the internet is a fantastic tool for learning; all of humanity's knowledge is there – though admittedly *various versions* of that knowledge! Immediate, desk-based access to the internet is not so relevant in primary schools, but for secondary schools, the question can be whether the school should provide devices such as Chromebooks or iPads for every pupil.

Some schools allow pupils to use their own smart phones as a way of researching on the internet during lessons for research. Here are five reasons why I think pupils having their smart phones with them during the school day is problematic.

1. In 2023, psychologists[1] working with victims and perpetrators of sexual abuse in schools in Devon and Cornwall asked their clients the question, "When and where do you most often access pornography?" The top answer, with a 60+% score was, "On my phone, on the playground at break time." I am not sure I need to give any more reasons for why phones in school are a bad idea, but I will!
2. Messaging between pupils during the school day creates a backchannel of remarks about teachers, events, the school, and each other. That then continues into the evening, night, weekends, and holidays – and it simply never lets up. Having time away from their phones is a much needed and welcome break from the pressure that comes with too much digital communication. Some teachers argue that when phones are not allowed, pupils will find sneaky ways around the rule: a dummy phone or clever concealment. In reality, they don't do that for the simple reason that there is no point in having a phone if they're the only person in their social circle with one – they have no one to message!
3. Filming teachers, filming arguments, filming fights, filming pranks, filming in toilets or changing rooms – these are all too tempting for some pupils, and entirely inappropriate. Any such film posted on social media is massively corrosive of pride in the school.
4. The ability of a pupil to phone or text home when they have been told off or feel unjustly treated causes havoc and undermines the authority of the adults in the school. On a more mundane level, watch how quickly, when it starts snowing, pupils tell their parents the school is closing when no such announcement has been made!
5. Most of all, pupils don't *need* their phones. Teachers are perfectly capable of working round the lack of instant access to apps or the internet; it is certainly not worth the sacrifice to standards of behaviour and respect.

Some schools have phone policies that state that pupils may retain possession of their phones during the school day, but they must be switched off and hidden at all times. This is a poorly judged policy which doesn't work; the temptation to turn the phone on and use it in all the ways described is too great. Threats to confiscate the phone for a day/a week are undermined by angry phone calls from parents who don't recognise the right of the school to confiscate anything and argue – not unreasonably – that the phone is a safety device for the journey to and from school.

In my view, the only sensible policy is to require pupils to hand in their phones at the beginning of the day or put them in a pouch which can only be unlocked by a teacher. It's pretty simple, really.

## Note

1 https://www.bbfc.co.uk/about-us/news/children-see-pornography-as-young-as-seven-new-report-finds?t

# 17 Managing teaching and the curriculum

A few years ago, I tried to launch a new 6th form at the school I led. The idea was to provide an alternative to the more conventional 6th form provision in the area which was already excellent, varied, and comprehensive. 6th formers would have the chance to do re-take GCSEs in English and Maths, and study for a BTech at level 2 or 3. The main selling point was going to be the KIP lessons – 'Knowledge is Power'. The idea was to focus on the world of work and help students develop enough skills and knowledge across a wide spectrum of topics to be able to succeed. This would include knowing how to hold casual or formal conversations which would quickly establish trust. There would be lessons to fill in gaps in basic cultural and political understanding, such as knowing the difference between Bach, Beethoven, and Mozart, and being able to describe the difference between left-wing and right-wing politics, communism and fascism, and so on.

Sadly, though all the adults I spoke to about the project thought it was a great idea and filled an important gap for those pupils at the lower end of the GCSE attainment spectrum, the potential students were only interested in how many actual qualifications were on offer, so no one signed up.

Though the project failed, it reflected my view that what is taught in schools does not prepare young people well for adult life and the world of work – especially the low attainers. Curriculum design across all schools is driven by the examination system and regulation, both of which are heavily controlled by central government. But there is a layer of educational purpose that lies beneath the siloed subject areas and exam specifications, which can be manipulated to be make education more relevant and universally applicable. Let me explain.

We want pupils to be the following:

- curious
- ambitious in their learning
- self-motivated
- willing participants
- reflective
- unafraid to fail
- articulate
- empowered and autonomous learners

Schools can support pupils to be all of those things through an emphasis on the competencies that underpin effective learning. To achieve that, the pedagogy being practised in every classroom needs to be scaffolded by the vision and values of the school as promoted by the Headteacher. Here are some examples.

## Learned helplessness

Because I taught Year 7 in an all-through school, I was able to witness the attitudes to learning as they were influenced by the primary section. I found that there was a distinct sense of 'learned helplessness' in some of the Year 7 pupils. They tended to refer to the teacher (in this case, me) for every little detail when performing a learning task in lessons. There were times when I was inundated with unneeded queries such as the following:

- "Should I put my name at the top of this?" (The worksheet had a box which said *"Put your name here"*)
- "Shall I turn the page over?" (It was clearly marked *PTO*)
- "Question 3 has two parts. Should I answer both?"

And so on. These queries were also characterised by mindless repetition – even though a question had been asked and answered, several more pupils would lodge the same query.

So, I created new rules for Year 7s to follow. When asking them to complete a worksheet, I told the class – given that I had already explained the worksheet very carefully – that, collectively, they must not ask more than two questions. Within seconds, a hand would shoot up and a pupil would ask something like "What happens if we ask more than two questions?" and "What is an unneeded question?"

I would then say, "Well, there's two unneeded questions right there – sorry, none left; let's get on with it."

A directive was given to all staff in the primary part of the school to consider very carefully how to promote pupils' autonomy in their learning. Teachers were asked to witness and support the discomfort of pupils as they struggled to solve 'the problem' for themselves, and not always intervene to fix things: "Try to work it out for yourself. I know you can do it."

## Oracy

Visiting dozens of schools each year, I am struck by the huge variation in pupils' oracy skills. Very few schools place an emphasis on developing pupils' basic skill and confidence in expressing themselves orally without stumbling, feeling embarrassed or fearing humiliation. Yet it is such a vital attribute, and one which opens many doors. Being confidently articulate improves access to better questions and deeper learning; it allows pupils to engage with philosophical discussion and also to develop identity. It is through the spoken word that their personal sense of self is established and witnessed.

There are plenty of ways to improve oracy, and simply asking teachers to maximise opportunities during lessons is straightforward. Schools could go further by requiring every pupil to present at least once a week, whether that is in a lesson, registration or even in an assembly, for which double kudos. Many pupils are naturally shy and are therefore reluctant to speak up in class, let alone make presentations in front of peers. Those pupils need the school's robust support to overcome an oral reticence which may otherwise prove to be a major barrier to lifelong success, socially and at work. PE, music, and drama are such vital subject areas because they contain regular moments when pupils are required to perform. There is no reason why, with a little imagination, every other subject should not follow suit. From the pre-schooler whose vocabulary is inherently limited, through to the adolescent boy who has adopted grunting as his main means of communication, all pupils can benefit from being more articulate and more confident in their oracy.

## Careers

Careers education has been statutory since 2018, but many schools only really pay lip service to it. If a school buys into the Gatsby framework (Gatsby.org.uk) – both literally and philosophically – then it can move steadily forward until the mission statement *"Preparing children for the world of work"* actually means something.

Careers education starts in Reception and is no less relevant then than it is in Year 13. The emphasis is not just on choosing a career; it's also on oracy, inter-personal skills, how to be liked, how to network, how to influence people in the right way . . . and *charm*. I remember asking a group of boys in Year 10 whether they thought charm was important. None of them did, and I felt like muttering, "Yes, it shows," but I didn't.

Showing even a modicum of charm is something many pupils struggle with. Put it this way: how often is the Head Girl/Boy chosen because they make the adults smile?

Careers education, a bit like safeguarding, is the responsibility of every teacher. Every teacher can emphasise the skills and knowledge base their subject area is contributing to the future success of a career path. It need not be a waged career path; some pupils may choose as adults to be stay-at-home parents or develop their own intellect through further study.

Embedding careers education into the curriculum ensures that the education the school provides is unequivocally focused on preparing for life.

## Meta-cognition

I have always loved the idea of promoting meta-cognition in my pupils, right from the early days when I taught clarinet and saxophone one-to-one. We have known for a long time that it is as important to teach pupils *how* to learn as it is to teach subject knowledge has been around a long time – yet it is rare to see this in action in the classroom.

I became frustrated with myself for asking teachers to promote meta-cognition because I realised I was being too vague. What is meta-cognition, and indeed, what is knowledge? If pupils don't fully understand what knowledge is, then how can we expect them to acquire it? For that matter, if the ways people learn can be defined in multiple ways, how can pupils choose the most effective one?

## What is knowledge?

The first words of my master's degree study in education were, "The nature of knowledge is contested." I then spent three years studying the multiple ways in which we try to define knowledge, all of which proved the fulsome truth of that opening statement. Many years later, when I was trying to find holistic ways to improve the studying experiences of pupils in Key Stage 4, it struck me that the objective of GCSEs is to **acquire knowledge** and the fact that a quick definition of knowledge is not readily available only makes study harder. The same can equally be said of Key Stage 2 Standard Assessment Tests (SATs). I reasoned that if we could define knowledge simply and memorably, then the objectives of studying would be clear and that would help everyone learn more effectively.

Inspired by various staff room conversations with teachers from different subject disciplines, I came up with the following, which is called **Learning 123**.

Knowledge can be defined in the following three ways:

1. FACTS. Facts are straightforward, often one-word answers to a question. For example, the capital of France is Paris. Facts form the basis of wider and more sophisticated definitions of what it means to be 'knowledgeable'. They are the bedrock of understanding and knowledgeability. Despite the scorn Charles Dickens poured on Mr Gradgrind in *Hard Times*, facts are undeniably useful and need to be 'known' – and not just Googled when needed.
2. PROCESSES. Processes are facts joined together and understood. For example, *how plants grow* is a piece of process knowledge. We know that plants need light, water, and nutrients. Water helps absorb nutrients from the soil and light converts the nutrients into the energy needed for the plant to grow.
3. SKILLS. Skills are *how to . . .* knowledge, like playing the piano or kicking a ball in the air instead of along the ground. Skills are divided into two categories: **MENTAL** skills, like being able to work out a circumference from a radius, and **PHYSICAL** skills, like how to catch a ball.

So far, so good? I ran this mini-thesis past a distinguished professor of psychology who had studied for 40 years the ways we understand and process meaning in the domains of language and concepts, and he was impressed. In fact, he said that the model, though 'top level' thinking (i.e. there is much more to say going underneath these definitions) could not be faulted.

Emboldened and mindful that my Year 11s would still look at me as if I was from another planet, I thought I would have a crack at learning. What is learning, and how does it take place?

Learning takes place when you do the following:

1. REVISIT. In order to make something *stick* in your memory and make the learning long-lasting, you need to *recall* it. The more complex the knowledge you want to learn, the more often you have to recall it. That's where homework tasks and regular mini tests are useful, constantly requiring pupils to revisit their knowledge.
2. USE. A great way to make your learning *stick* and become useful is to *use* the knowledge. This is perhaps the hardest learning technique to deploy, but if a pupil can find a reason to use their knowledge, it becomes more stable and sticks more. The following are two ways this can be achieved:
    a. Ask pupils to explain new learning to their parent(s) and ask parents to set aside time each evening, perhaps over a meal, to listen to these explanations.
    b. Flip the roles in class – make the pupil the teacher and ask them to explain their new knowledge to the class.
3. PRACTICE. In order to consolidate and improve your *how to . . .* knowledge, you need to practise it. You become *skilled* at playing the piano through practice. Practice usually involves slow, deliberate, correct repetition.

## Is educational research useful?

In the 2010s, it became popular for teachers and curriculum leaders to seek ways to improve pedagogy by reading research that showed which methods were most effective and which least. In part this was prompted by the best-selling book *Visible Learning*[1] by John Hattie. Hattie synthesised more than 800 meta-analyses of the many pedagogical techniques used in the classroom, as well as other influences on learners, such as their home environment. His book built on an existing desire to follow the world of medicine in using research to find the best way to do anything involving humans and change. The Department for Education got involved, as well, and the movement was driven forward by researchers such as Sam Freedman to the point where it became a stated government goal for teachers to become researchers in their own right.

Whilst Hattie's work prompted useful debates about the best ways to teach, there has always been a lingering doubt in my mind about the validity of evidenced-based strategies. In the millions of bits of data that Hattie drew from, where was the control group for each individual pedagogical technique? In other words, how can you isolate one technique from another, given that at any one point, pupils are being exposed to multiple techniques?

On the whole, measuring the effectiveness of medical treatment is straightforward compared to measuring learning outcomes; the patient is either cured or not, and usually one set of treatments is administered at a time. Learning, on the other hand, is much harder to measure. Is the acquired knowledge we are trying to measure deep and lasting, or is it shallow and designed for regurgitation in a test? *Where* and *when* does learning take place – contemporaneously, or during a piece of homework designed to prompt reflection and consolidation? *How* does learning happen – there are many theories, so which one is right? Is learning different in the maths classroom from the English classroom – or PE or music?

In 2024, new research[2] emerged which, ironically, debunked the idea that evidence-based pedagogy was any better than using common sense. Sally Riordan from University College, London, looked at multiple randomised studies that measured the impact of evidence-based teaching methods and found little or no impact. Her report concluded that "[w]e don't have enough evidence to be confident that evidence should always be our first port of call."

## Conclusion

It can feel like the shape and content of the curriculum will probably never change significantly and will remain frustratingly tangential to the need to prepare pupils for adult life. It can seem to the pupils that much of what they learn is not specifically useful for them in their current or future lives, but an emphasis on the core competencies, skills, and guided attitudes will help each pupil succeed in their chosen path.

## Notes

1 John Hattie, *Visible Learning*. Pub Routledge, 2008.
2 theconversation.com, April 2024.

# 18 Managing non-teaching staff

We have spent some time considering the best way to manage teaching staff; how to get the best from non-teaching staff is vital, too. Whether or not the school has a site manager, finance officer or some other form of line management for non-teaching staff, the Headteacher is still ultimately responsible for how this team of people contributes to the running of the school.

Depending on the size and type of school, there will be the following:

- Reception Office staff, who often have additional administrative tasks including admissions, attendance register, and some aspects of compliance.
- Site staff, who are variously responsible for caretaking, opening, and locking up the school, alarm systems, maintenance, grounds, some decoration, and compliance in relation to legionella, fire regulations, and health and safety.
- Cleaners, who are sometimes in-house and sometimes employed by a contractor. Either way, there is still some management needed regarding access, DBS checks, performance management, and so on.
- Finance staff, who also support the work of the Top Layer and might also deal with lettings.
- Marketing, development and communications officers, who sometimes sit on SLT and therefore contribute to discussions about vision and values.
- PAs to SLT, who sometimes also double up as Clerk to the Governors.
- Technicians supporting IT, science, food technology, design and technology, and art.
- School Nurse, whose remit can be surprisingly wide, involving liaising with many outside agencies.
- Catering staff, with plenty of their own compliance issues.
- Miscellaneous others such as minibus drivers, data analysts, and attendance officers.

Headteachers are nearly always former teachers and Deputy Heads, and their experience will not usually have prepared them for the task of managing the non-teaching team. As we can see from this list, it is a big team with a big slice of the budget allocated to their wages; getting the team working well is no mean task. In a boarding school, the list is even longer.

The line management structure and job descriptions of the non-teaching team usually evolve over time. In other words, 'the way it works' is rarely the result of careful and comprehensive strategic thinking; it is normally an organic drift towards the status quo. That is because many non-teaching tasks can be done by anyone with an aptitude and willingness, so roles are often combined under one multi-aspect job description. Typically, tasks tend to gravitate to the most talented employees or to those employees who want more hours, and this can create a rather idiosyncratic diagram of workflow. That is further complicated by the resignation of an employee who wore several 'hats', and the school's quest to find someone to perform the same role. Perhaps a replacement is found, but the way the various tasks are performed as they appear on the job description is not replicated to the same level of quality as by the previous incumbent. It all quite quickly becomes a jumble and quite chaotic.

This is no way to run a school! The Headteacher may well be the only person with a sufficiently clear overview to be able to unpick the mess and put it right. It starts with an analysis of the tasks that need to be done and an understanding of how much time and budget should be allocated to each one. That enables the Headteacher to decide on the ideal way in which each task can be performed, and how line management should operate. This has to be done dispassionately with absolutely no regard, in the first instance, to who is currently performing those tasks. Then the ideal scenario is mapped over the existing workflow structure to see what compromises need to be made. Some redundancies, additional training, and negotiations over job descriptions may follow, but the end result will be a reset which produces better results within a tightly justified budget.

All this is especially relevant for the new Headteacher, who often inherits an ants' nest of non-teaching protocols based almost entirely on the personalities and needs of the personnel, rather than the needs of the school. The best time to reorganise, therefore, is in the first year of Headship. Reviews need to happen any time someone leaves their non-teaching post, to see if there are opportunities to increase efficiency. There are also many reasons why non-teaching roles change over time as new regulations are applied and targets in the strategic vision of the school are met.

## Finding ways to motivate

Much of the work of the non-teaching team can be deemed to be limited in scope and ambition compared to the team that works directly with pupils. For example, a music teacher might be motivated by the prospect of growing a department until nearly every pupil is in a choir or playing an instrument. But no such pathway of growth exists for many non-teaching staff: the cleaners will clean well, the caretakers will lock up on time, the auditors will approve the work of the finance team – and that's it. Motivation to go the extra mile is hard to find because the extra mile doesn't really exist or at least is hard to define. It is therefore important that the Headteacher – as the ultimate line manager – finds ways to motivate, inspire, and acknowledge the hard work of these employees. Popping into the kitchens regularly to offer praise and support, thanking the IT team for fixing the internet quickly, and taking a detailed interest in systems to record the attendance register are all ways in which members of the non-teaching team can feel validated and appreciated.

Leading non-teaching staff will take up a surprising amount of time, even in a well-run school. Despite this work feeling tangential to teaching and learning, it is still an important part of the vision and values that underpin the way the school is run.

In the next chapter we will take a dive into the most significant part of the non-teaching team: the Finance Department.

# 19 Money and how to use it

The person who has decisive control over the money effectively runs the school, so it is worthwhile for a Headteacher to put time and thought into getting this right.

## Is the Finance Department appropriately staffed?

I was once chasing payment of an invoice from a school and spoke on the phone to the person in charge of 'accounts payable'. She apologised for the late payment, remarking that "No one ever tells us what they are buying" and that she had 245 un-opened emails, most of which contained new invoices. In other words, she was overwhelmed – and that, in my experience, is not uncommon. When the Finance Department is under-staffed (or the staff are not sufficiently competent and/or trained), it can undermine the morale of all other staff. Teachers request resources which don't get ordered despite ordering protocols being followed, emails from parents about fees for extra-curricular activities go unanswered, caterers' requests for replacement machinery take months to be actioned. Then the Headteacher needs to prepare management accounts for the Top Layer, the information is incomplete and carries many riders and anomalies. Again, this is no way to run school!

Here are some basic strategies that can help.

Is the **software package** used by the Finance Department suitable for the size and scale of the school's turnover? Many schools spend a significant amount of money on accounting software whose capacity is often much greater than is needed and which is also not fully understood by the users. Being bold enough to swap to a simpler, more appropriate system can be an excellent first step.

Does the school use **purchase order numbers**? This is controversial because I have yet to work in a school, including the ones I led, which use them effectively. The idea is that anyone making an order of any kind – whether the caretaker buying new keys, the chef buying food, or a French teacher buying new resources – *everyone* must request a purchase order (PO) number first. The person ordering the goods or services describes briefly what is being bought and – vitally – which budget the expenditure should be allocated to. This means that when the invoice comes in – quoting the PO number – the Finance Department can: a) quickly gain approval from the person making the order, b) correctly assign the payment to the right budget, and c) make the payment quickly and within the 30-day limit. In order that a PO number system works properly, it must be made a requirement by the Headteacher, who must be prepared to get cross with people who don't follow protocol.

In groups of schools, such as Multi-Academy Trusts, this has become a central plank in strategies to stay on top of accurate budget allocation, which in turn leads to accurate management accounts.

## Budgeting and the timetable

No matter the size of the school or how it is funded, the Headteacher will have at least some responsibility for creating a budget. This is normally done about 6-9 months ahead of the new academic year and requires some clear thinking. How money is allocated is often a very visible way of demonstrating the school's commitment to its values and vision. The time to create the budget is also, therefore, the time to start the process of writing a new timetable. That starts with a staffing analysis, which is where someone, usually from SLT, decides how many teachers are needed and which teacher is going to stand in front of which class. This analysis changes every year because some teachers want more or fewer hours, or there may be a change to the number or configuration of forms in each year group. Staffing requirements are never static, and this is the part of the timetabling process that can only be done – or at least signed off by the Headteacher because it has budgeting implications for the year ahead.

## Budgets that match reported cost centres

The Headteacher should be the one to allocate the financial resources of the school to the various budgets the school decides on. For example, there will be a budget for teaching salaries and another for non-teaching salaries. The cost of food will be separated from the cost of the kitchen staff wages. By creating a granulated map of projected expenditure in the form of budgets, the school can monitor and control its money. However, when it comes to the final analysis of outcomes at the end of the financial year, auditors tend to amalgamate budgets to create overarching cost centres. So, to use this example, the figures ultimately put together by the auditors, and therefore voted on formally by the Top Layer, show wages as a single cost – thus precluding the opportunity to scrutinise the differences between teaching and non-teaching wages. Requiring a detailed budget-by-budget report from auditors makes sense of the whole exercise.

## The budget is a guide not a limit

If the requirement to stick within the budget is too strict, it can limit opportunities to make use of money when and where it might be most impactful. For example, the local supplier of laptops has a special offer if you buy ten or more. Buying these devices would blow the IT budget for this year, but it is clearly a sensible decision to make because it saves money in the long run. As long as any over-expenditure is explained and justified, it's fine; the budget figure is just a guide and should not be allowed to get in the way of making sensible and prudent decisions.

Use **management accounts**. Management accounts are simply a way of monitoring income and expenditure on a regular basis – usually once a month, or least every half term. The Finance Officer will undertake the task of totalling money spent in each cost centre and comparing that with expectation. For example, the school will have a budget for fuel for the mini-buses. Each month, a running total of how much has been spent will appear as a percentage of the allocated budget – halfway through the year, we would expect half the allocated budget to have been used – but matching expenditure against expectation needs to be contextualised. For example, we will need to bear in mind that May is the time of year for residential and camping trips, which takes up a lot more of the fuel budget than in other months. The monitoring of this cost centre is put into the context of the school's knowledge of how the money is usually spent. To help with that thinking, the running total from the previous year's management accounts sits in a column next to the current year for comparison.

None of this is especially hard to achieve if everyone is competent and not overwhelmed in their role. And yet in my 18 years as Headteacher, I never quite achieved a set of management accounts that was reasonably accurate and useful – something always got in the way.

It is important for the Headteacher to have the courage to question the ways financial data is generated, interpreted, and presented. It is not uncommon for the professionals trained in accounting to present management accounts in a format that is – dare I say – *designed* to obscure. When challenged about the lack of transparency, they hide behind jargon and make the non-professionals feel out of their depth. But actually, finance can be and *should* be pretty simple. How much money are we spending? Are we spending more than we should? How much money do we have, and how is that allocated in the budget? That means that if there's a new project to be funded, or if there is an unexpected cost – like the boiler breaking down – the Headteacher and Top Layer can quickly and easily work out what to do.

## Profit and loss accounts vs cash accounts (and a bit about depreciation)

It can be useful to make a distinction between a school's **cash** accounting and the **profit and loss** (P&L) accounts. Cash, as the name implies, tells us what money is actually there, the incomes, and the expenditures. P&L is a more complex and legalistic document used at the year-end to describe the complete financial picture regarding assets, tax liability, depreciation, and so on. Generally speaking, the cash account is what the Headteacher needs to keep their eye on – though I'm sure that any accountants reading this will throw their hands up in horror!

The appearance of **depreciation** in the P&L accounts can be confusing. Here is a simplified explanation. Imagine you buy a minibus for £30,000; in terms of how much the school is worth, the money in the bank has been converted into an asset, known as a tangible fixed asset. It's no longer £30,000 showing in the bank – it's now a shiny new bus parked in front of the school. However, the minibus will have lost value after a year – let's say 10% of the price paid – and so the tangible fixed asset is now worth only £27,000. The accounts need to reflect this loss in value as a cost, and so the expenditure column of the P&L will show this as depreciation: £3,000. The annual P&L accounts will continue to show an expenditure of 10% of the value of the minibus for the next 10 years. But that, of course, is not a cash figure; it's an accounting figure. The school hasn't actually *spent* £3,000 – it has just lost £3,000 in the overall value of its assets.

When I was producing the budget for the coming year for the Top Layer, I would add in the depreciation figure but show the final expected surplus *with* and also *without* depreciation. That seemed like a sensible way to satisfy both my interest in the cash and the accountants' interest in exactitude.

## Don't skimp on maintenance

It can be tempting to delay a refurb or make a corridor last another year before redecorating it. These are false economies and postpone the cost of maintenance, which may end up costing the school more. Similarly, when it comes to purchasing goods which need to last, don't buy cheap – buy once.

## Decrease expenditures and/or increase income

It's rare that a school will profess to having 'enough' money, and so ways to save or make more money are always welcome. The following are some ideas:

Renegotiate bank loans.
Borrow from the bank.
Utilise parent goodwill and labour.
Develop or re-develop the Parent Association.
Review all subscriptions/service contracts.
Sweat the assets – introduce or expand lettings.
An appeal to raise money, utilising alumni goodwill.
Reduce energy costs:

> 'Go Green' Campaign; e.g., put the staff room water heater on a timer.
> Source green funding to change all light fittings and/or fit photovoltaic (PV) cells.
> Put thermostats on radiators.
> Fit movement sensors for lights.
> Lag heating pipes.
> Service the boiler properly.
> Shut down the use of energy at weekends and holidays.
> Does the air conditioning need to be so fierce in the server room?

Zero budgeting: Make every budget holder justify every pound they request.
Examine every cost centre for waste:

> Is the school getting value for money from the MIS?
> Guiding the IT strategy: are the best people involved?
> Review communication channels: Is the school wasting money by having too many?

Then recruit more pupils by making the school the best it can be, e.g.:

> Improve the visuals, lines of sight, lick of paint, kerb appeal, first impressions, fencing, grass, loos, minibus.
> Improve the smell of the school, especially for Open Days.
> Is the school's SEND provision the best it can be?
> Track all potential families from the first enquiry.
> Review show-round and Open Day procedures.
> Invite new pupils' former teachers for tea.
> Send a postcard home after each show-round.
> Review the school's unique selling points: Have they changed? Survey the current parents.
> Review overlaps with competitors and make the school's offer unique for the area.
> Improve the school's local reputation by winning things, such as local music festivals, sporting fixtures and tournaments, or academic competitions, e.g., essay writing and public speaking.
> Review overall marketing strategy.
> Grandparent Day.

Summer Fayre for the community in order to increase footfall.
Increase awareness of the school: carnival floats, care home visits, charities.
Work with feeder schools.
Emphasise and enhance the school's unique offers.
Modernise and innovate.

## Conclusion

Managing money is often the aspect of running a school that teachers approaching and aspiring to Headship find hardest to grasp and gain experience of.

My advice:

- Don't be bamboozled by the accountants. Ask if you don't understand, then keep asking until you do understand. Then be bold in presenting the figures in a way that you feel is clear.
- Claim and retain as much influence over the money as the Top Layer will grant you – then ask for more!

# 20  School development planning

Much hinges on the SDP because a school is like a shark – it can never stay still for fear of sinking. Depending on the stipulations of the latest inspection framework, the SDP is scrutinised and regarded by inspectors as a key document. Whatever weaknesses a school may have, if they are on the agenda to be repaired and strengthened, then that helps. The projects on the SDP demonstrate that the school leadership, in conjunction with the Top Layer, have audited the school's strengths and weaknesses, and that the audit has informed the way forward. The SDP may also contain innovations and changes in practice that are simply good ideas, regardless of what the school is currently doing.

A key question to ask, as the SDP is created, is, "What will be the **drivers for improvement**?" The answer to that question is not only a barometer of the Head's commitment to continuous improvement but is also something that all child-facing members of staff should be very familiar with.

## How to create an effective SDP

There are many misconceptions about SDPs. First, they don't have to be annual documents. The projects on the plan may be implemented in a term or three years – rarely do they fit neatly into an academic year. The idea that SDP should be reviewed, refreshed, and re-released at a set time of year is not useful: it leads to plans that are tokenistic and of little real value as drivers of change.

Instead, the SDP will have its own natural life span. That might mean that a refreshed SDP will be published somewhere between 9 months and 18 months after the previous one.

The spontaneous nature of the re-emergence of the SDP will give each re-launch a sense of relevance and interest.

## Short and pithy

To maximise impact, it is a good idea to restrict the projects on the SDP to no more than four. It's also sensible to consider creating improvements to different aspects of the school's operation. For instance, one project might be about pedagogical practice in the classroom, such as implementing a 'hands down' policy and allowing 'thinking time' in question-and-answer sessions. Another might be to integrate a new learning platform, ensuring that all teachers are making good use of this investment. A third might relate to pastoral care and involve a new project that listens to the pupils' opinions about the safest and least safe areas of the school and local community.

The SDP should *always* focus solely on teaching and learning; a different document will deal with capital projects, refurbishments, new investment in IT, etc. That document might be called a 'strategic' plan, but making it distinct from the SDP is crucial. If the SDP has extraneous items not focused on teaching and learning, then many staff will ignore it.

The process of populating the SDP, as we explored in the chapter on leadership styles (Chapter 14), is a matter for consultation. In the early days of a Headship, lots of consultation will be appreciated, whereas once the new leadership has been established and trust has been built, staff will be largely content for new ideas to come from SLT.

Just because "it says it on the SDP" doesn't mean it will happen. The leadership team will have to persuade, incentivise, and possibly cajole the implementers. Therefore, the SDP will contain, along with a brief description of the project, a time scale, a leader (usually from SLT), the projected cost, and desired outcomes. This should, in my view, all fit on one side of a sheet of A4 paper.

**Measuring success**

Not all SDP projects are necessarily measurable – or at least it is not always useful to cite measurement criteria, because they can distort the intention behind the project. For example, if a school is looking to improve the relational cultures between boys, available strategies to measure success are limited to pupil surveys. Those surveys may not always be accurate, because there are many reasons why pupils may or may not choose to be honest on a survey. Instead, a qualitative measure is just as valuable and less intrusive. The desired outcome might simply be that the mood of the school has improved – that interactions between boys are observed to be more harmonious and less conflictual. The fact that there is no quantitative data does not matter. Projects involving relational cultures and interpretations of the school's ethos do not have to be measured in scientifically valid ways. Data is not always king!

Leading a school is a creative job with enormous scope for innovation and insightful strategies to help find those small incremental, marginal gains. Drawing up the next version of the SDP should be one of the most enjoyable and inspiring tasks in the life of the school.

# 21 Crisis management

Every crisis, by its very nature, is highly contextualised. Therefore, crisis planning has to be done on a very generic level, and there are two aspects:

- Understanding the structure of how a crisis can be best managed
- Crisis public relations (PR)

## How to structure the management of a crisis

Without some training and agreed ways of working, managing a crisis can quickly become chaotic – only adding to the crisis itself. When a 'bad' thing has happened, it is the job of the leadership of the school to try to ensure that the 'bad' thing is not made worse by poor decision-making, confused communications, and panic.

Leadership teams can train staff in the Gold/Silver/Bronze (strategic/tactical/operational) command structure. Here's a brief overview:

The Headteacher would normally assume the role of **Gold Command**, unless they are absent or incapacitated. Gold Command develops the **overall strategy**, determining priorities such as protecting human life, maintaining calm, and ensuring the continuity of critical services and communications.

**Silver Command:** One person – perhaps a member of SLT and appointed by Gold Command – creates **tactical plans** to ensure ongoing safety.

**Bronze Command:** Most staff would **carry out** the tactical plan, for example, aspects such as evacuations, lockdowns, rescue operations, liaising with emergency services, supporting parental pick-ups, etc.

The most effective training is to allocate some time with all staff, perhaps on an In Service Training day, to act out a pre-conceived scenario and see how it goes. The Gold Command system is effective, and can be used in smaller moments of crisis, too. For example, in a PE lesson, a pupil suffers a dislocated knee joint which is extremely painful and causes her to panic and scream in pain. PE staff would do well to allocate Gold, Silver, and Bronze roles to adults around them to ensure the best outcome for the victim and all the other pupils. Without the concept of Gold Command, it can be very challenging to create a structured response to any crisis. Simply role-playing scenarios with staff can be very valuable.

## Getting the PR right

The way to plan the PR side of things can be more specific and practical. Planning PR will not only save time but will also provide the leadership team with good quality material and resources at a time when thinking skills may be compromised by ongoing trauma.

DOI: 10.4324/9781003517825-24

The SLT can therefore create a 'crisis folder' which will contain pithy lists of things to remember, such as the following:

- who needs to be told
- how to log into the school text alert system using a phone and 5G
- lists of contacts
- pre-written email texts
- and so on

The folder is the best way to ensure that nothing is missed; everything counts, and a small omission can not only lead to the crisis deepening but will also be the subject of justified criticism when the review is undertaken.

Train the Headteacher in how to talk to journalists. Leaders need to learn how to avoid saying things that might inflame a situation.

As the immediate crisis passes and the school moves into the aftermath phase, be sure to provide proper support to the marketing and communications team. While senior teachers can oversee looking after the pupils, the Headteacher needs to retain an overview of all the teams in the organisation.

Individuals, post-crisis, may appear to be doing fine and then suddenly collapse and struggle to cope. The Headteacher might also experience this, so planning needs to be in place to step in for the Head if necessary. Despite that contingency, the school ideally needs the Headteacher to stay on top of things and remain calm and confident – so planning for personal support is also vital.

We all hope it never happens, but some form of crisis will *probably* occur during the tenure of each Headteacher. How the school comes through the crisis is a true test of leadership.

# 22 Crisis management - A case study

This chapter tells the story of a Deputy Head who took his own life and what had happened to cause that. This is a personal experience. All the details are in a report published by the Independent Police Complaints Commission and are therefore already in the public domain.

It was the summer of 2014 and the school had just turned a corner in terms of pupil recruitment. The Deputy Head, Martin Goldberg, had had a busy holiday re-writing academic groupings to incorporate an influx of 50-plus pupils who were joining the school unexpectedly.

On September 9, I was at a sector meeting in the evening, away from my hometown, when Goldberg rang me. I couldn't take the call but checked his voice message a few minutes later. He asked me to ring him urgently, which I did, but he didn't pick up – neither then nor the numerous times I rang him throughout the rest of the evening. I called the other Deputy Head, who couldn't raise him either. We decided to leave it for now.

In the morning, Goldberg did not arrive for the morning briefing with staff; this was concerning. A couple of colleagues, who knew where he lived, volunteered to go to his house to check that he was okay.

Half an hour later, one of them rang me. She said they could see signs of distress when they looked through the letter box and had called the police. The police found Goldberg hanging in his garage and called an ambulance. When I arrived on the scene, I was greeted by a police officer who told me that doctors were still working on him but that the situation was grave. The policeman then told me that two officers had visited Goldberg at 6:00pm the previous evening and had asked to perform a scan of his computer for obscene material. Information had come to light that he had purchased a video some ten years previously that contained images of naked children. Inside the house, Goldberg had attempted to destroy computers and memory cards, setting fire to some.

I returned to school and began to manage the ensuing situation. As I met with senior deputies, I received a call from the police saying that Goldberg had died. I decided to inform staff immediately.

I had reviewed the annual insurance policy only a few days before, so I was aware that the school was entitled to claim £10,000 in PR cover. I got in touch with the insurers, and a man from a PR company rang me a couple of hours later. He was very reassuring and had already done a lot of background work on the school and Goldberg. He met with the Governors and me every day for the next week; his input was central to ensuring the school handled the situation as well as we could.

The three weeks that followed were the toughest of my career. As the police undertook a forensic examination of Goldberg's computers and digital footprint, we held our breath that his crimes would be limited to that one video purchase. They were not. Investigators found images and videos of semi-naked boys taken in the school's changing rooms.

At this point, only Governors and SLT knew why Goldberg had taken his own life, and it was incredibly hard to manage the positive memories that circulated about him in the staff room. Staff were speculating on what hidden state of mental health might have caused him to take his own life.

One teacher remarked, "Perhaps we will just never know what happened or why he killed himself."

I replied, "Yes, but perhaps we also need to allow for the possibility that that is not the case..."

Over the three weeks between his death and the public announcement of what had happened, police Gold Command required a tight circle of trust, which was restricted to the police, the school, and the Local Authority. This was to ensure that the police had time to investigate the full extent of Goldberg's crimes before the story was given to the media. Police Gold Command also demanded that I alone attend these meetings, and although I protested that the Chair of Governors was entitled to be – and *should* be – there, I was overruled. I regret that I didn't trust my own professional and personal instincts, because his insistence was wrong. I felt very isolated.

Things came to a head just a few days before the conclusion of the investigation. I arrived at a meeting to discuss how the breaking news of Goldberg's story would be managed and was held up in the lobby, meaning I walked in a few minutes late through no fault of my own. The meeting had clearly been going on for some time, because everyone had used coffee cups in front of them. There were also many additional people from different organisations in attendance – not the usual people from the circle of trust I was expecting to see. I challenged why these additional people were there but was pushed back. During the meeting, representing the school on my own, with 15 others from the police and Local Authority, I was sneered at and put down. Blame for the incident seemed to be swinging towards the school.

I have never been so angry, before or since. The next day, I broke down before I could get into the staff briefing, so I called for a trusted colleague to help me. She was great and calmed me down; we called the Governors in for more moral support while I regained my composure. I decided to ring the police Gold Command there and then. Without raising my voice for a single moment, I told him how furious I was with him, how I felt bullied, manipulated, and victimised. I warned him that the school would go its own way in terms of public announcements unless the police amended its stance immediately.

My controlled counterattack worked, and from that moment on, the police softened their position.

With a few days to go before the police were due to go public, I sought solace and advice from a close family member. I was close to despair, feeling that the day of the announcement would be carnage and that the existential threat to the school was very real. He listened to my story and calmly pointed out that my only course of action was to continue to do what I had always done for the school – provide the best outcomes for the pupils and community. He said:

> "In a few weeks' time you want to be able to look back and say that you did the right thing at every stage; that you saved the school and looked after the families. If you focus

on that, you'll be able to lift your head right here, right now and start to strategise the best way forward."

His words resonated with me and inspired me; I overcame my despair, put aside my anger, and got on with the leadership role that would test me like nothing had before.

On the day the public were to find out had happened, the regional police commissioner decided to leak the news to the media early. Parents were due to be told at 9:30am and the press at 10:00am, but at 9:15am, no fewer than five major television channels arrived at the school with full outside broadcast vans and crew. The story the commissioner had leaked was that the police had a secret which they had been hiding for months. It turned out that the results of the operation which revealed Goldberg's purchase of obscene materials had been known to them for two years, and they had done nothing about it. Be that as it may, the media was camped outside the school, and they needed me to come and make a statement and answer questions.

As I prepared for this onslaught, my focus on the seriousness of the situation was blurred. The PR man stepped in. He said:

> "Right now, Andrew, you are looking to remain cheerful and in control by using 'gallows humour'. That's not going to work in front of the TV cameras. I need you to think as if you have just heard the news about Goldberg and feel that intense shock once again."

I suggested that we rehearse the possible questions and was therefore able to think through the best possible answers. Along with my wonderfully unflappable Marketing Officer, I came up with "The community is deeply angry, shocked and betrayed by this man's actions" as my opener.

It was a full-on day, announcing the news to staff then pupils, dealing with multiple media interviews, and talking to angry parents. The Governors were fully supportive and engaged and manned the phones all day, ensuring that parents understood that the pupils were safe and that we would come through this together. As I left that evening, I saw the ITV News still making reports live to camera outside the school gates.

Over the next few days, the local press repeatedly published grim headlines condemning the school from every possible angle. Despite this, my inbox filled with positive messages from parents. More than half the families specifically took the trouble to offer their unwavering support for me and the school. "I chose this school because I knew my child would be cared for and safe with you. Nothing in that thinking has changed." Most significantly, not a single child left the school as a result of these events.

Thinking back to what the family member had advised, I was confident that, with an extensive team, I had done the best I could.

## Conclusion

A few months after these events, I was invited to speak on the BBC's *Victoria Derbyshire Show*. One of the other guests was Jim Gamble, former Head of CEOP (Child Exploitation and Online Protection Centre). Encouragingly, he told me that they had used Goldberg as a case study in their training of field officers and that my "angry, shocked, and betrayed" words had been held up as an exemplary response from the Headteacher. He also emphasised how clever and devious people like Goldberg were in disguising their behaviours and that he was one of many men and women whose crimes had gone undetected for many years.

What we can draw from this experience is the following:

- Always be aware that the best interests of the police and other authorities will not always align with those of the school.
- Check your PR insurance cover, and know how to access it quickly.
- No matter how dire the situation, there is always a 'good job' to be done.

# 23 Assessment and data

When recruiting teachers, a challenging question is, "What is the relationship between assessment and learning?"

Before reading on, you might want to explore your own response to that question, because it is fundamental. Schools are focused on learning, and do lots of assessment, but what *is* the relationship between the two? Does the assessment of pupils' learning actually contribute to their overall education – and if so, how?

The answer given by a large majority of the interviewees was that by assessing what pupils have learned so far, the teacher can know how best to adjust the ongoing teaching input. Does the class need to revisit aspects of the topic, or can we now move on?

My response to this answer was to point out that it described the relationship between assessment and *teaching* but not between assessment and *learning*. Interviewees would often then become a little flustered and usually repeated their original response using different words.

As a pedagogical technique, *Assessment for Learning* has been around for many years, and it is therefore surprising that many teachers struggle to describe this relationship. I think the simplest and most powerful answer is the word **feedback**. A pupil is taught something and performs some form of exercise or test or takes part in a question-and-answer session. The teacher then delivers feedback to the pupil on how well they have taken on the teaching, and that feedback informs the pupil if they need to think again or congratulate themselves on their learning and store the new knowledge in their long-term memory. If most assessment is used in this way and for this purpose, it is a fundamentally important tool in the teacher's locker.

Another very simple way of expressing this is to describe assessment as either being 'summative' or 'formative'.

## Summative and formative assessment

**Summative assessment** data is usually generated as the result of a test and is a set of marks that can be added to the profile of that pupil, their class, their year group, and their school. This data is important and useful because it allows teachers and their line managers to know whether or not teaching is effective. It will allow the school to measure progress, plan for learning interventions, and identify the most effective teachers and their teaching techniques. Data generated through summative assessment tests is therefore a vital tool in running a school. However, it is much more useful to the school, line managers, and teachers than it is to the pupils. Also, in small schools – say, fewer than 100 pupils per year group – great care must be taken in using data to make comparative judgements. The data set is inherently too small to be reliable.

**Formative assessment**, on the other hand, is all about using whatever feedback techniques are most effective to enhance learning, give the pupils ownership over their knowledge acquisition, and motivate them. If that means giving marks or grades then so be it, but

DOI: 10.4324/9781003517825-26

as Wiliam and Black[1] point out, there are several problems with giving marks to every piece of pupil work without proper consideration.

## The problems with marking and grading

If a pupil performs a test of factual knowledge then it is appropriate and useful to award them with a mark – perhaps ten questions generate ten marks, so full marks is 10/10. That is appropriate in subjects which rely on factual knowledge – but even then, they are not that useful. In a maths test, pupils are encouraged to show their working; that means they can still get marks for the mathematical processes they deployed, even if a silly error created the wrong final answer. Similarly, in science, it is useful to know the periodic table, and marks can be given for a simple test of that knowledge. But properly *useful* learning quickly goes beyond that, to explore the understanding needed to make sense of this type of knowledge.

So far, so good – but when testing goes beyond factual knowledge and is applied to *processes* (defined as 'facts joined together and understood') and *skills* (knowing 'how to . . . '), marking and grading become less useful.

I was inspecting the Music Department of a secondary school where the Assessment Policy, which all teachers were required to follow, was that pupils should, wherever possible, be awarded marks out of 10 for the class or homework they completed. The music teacher showed me her mark book, and I pointed at a single data point where a pupil had been awarded 6. I asked the teacher whether the 6/10 had been given to a good musician who was underperforming or a non-musician who was clearly doing very well. The teacher was tearful as she proclaimed that the system just didn't work and was essentially unhelpful and meaningless. It felt to me as though the marks-out-of-10 policy had been created in order to create data which would enable the school to establish time-stamped markers for the measurement of progress, rather than aid the process of meaningful feedback which would promote better learning. This is a good example of an assessment policy that is more focused on *measuring* progress than how progress might be better achieved *using* assessment.

A teacher of A level English told me that she had taught a particular pupil all the way from Year 7 to Year 13. Towards the end of this seven-year stretch, the teacher asked the pupil why she never corrected the generic errors she was making, which the teacher had referenced in the written comments. The pupil had to admit that she had *never ever* read the written comments! On further exploration, it turned out that the teacher had always awarded a grade for her pupil's work which was based on a set of explicit criteria and then gone on to comment. Nonetheless, the pupil in question would always look at the grade first; if the grade was better than expected, then she felt there was no need to look at the comment, because she had outperformed her expectation. If the grade was as anticipated, then she felt the comments would only echo her own thoughts about the work and would not be useful. If the grade was below expectation, then she thought that reading the comments would be painful and she would rather just move on. The teacher was shocked, because she put great care into her comments and regarded them as an important way to feedback and improve learning. She wasn't wrong about that, but the grade was getting in the way – and it often does.

A more enlightened assessment and grading policy allows teachers to use **marks** when there is a factual test and only to use **grades** if they are tied to standardised testing or public exams such as SATs, GCSEs, or A levels but otherwise to resist using marks or grades altogether. To some senior leaders this may seem very radical, but it's not – it is simply allowing purposeful and useful assessment methods to be regarded as more important than gathering of data.

## Predicted grades

The process of predicting how a pupil will perform in public exams is complex, and different subject areas will deploy different strategies. Some subjects use scores achieved in tests taken to date and project those forward into a grade. Other subjects put more store by the mock exam result perhaps allowing a one grade uplift in the prediction to allow for further progress. Some subjects don't finish teaching the entire curriculum until a few days before the first exam, which makes predictions almost impossible. Some teachers will deliberately underestimate the grade to give the pupil a jolt to work harder; others go the other way and overestimate the grade to give the pupil encouragement. None of this would matter that much except that entry into 6th forms and further/higher education establishments is to some extent dependent on these predictions, and this can cause friction between the school and the pupils. To ease this friction, negotiations are sometimes entered into, for example:

Teacher: If you hand in all the homework and coursework you currently owe, and it shows a suitable standard, I will uplift the prediction.
[It seems to me that the teacher here has just allowed all their previous deadlines to be undermined. The pupil may well hand in all that work, and it may well *not* meet the standard – but that simply opens up new negotiations.]

Parent: You *have* to help me out here – these predictions are just not high enough for us to be able to apply to the university of our choice. Come on – what can be done . . . ?

Things can quickly become messy, especially when the results come in and the grade is, say, two below the prediction. The parent then argues, "But you told us they would get a grade *two* above that; what on earth went wrong?"

There is a scene in the film *Clueless*,[2] an American movie based on the Jane Austen novel *Emma*, in which Cher – the lead character, aged 16 – shows her father her end-of-term report card in which her grades have risen dramatically. He quizzes her as to why her grades have improved so much, asking her if she did a lot of extra study. The reality is that Cher had persuaded, manipulated, and bribed her way to better grades. She replies that the new grades were "[t]otally based on my powers of persuasion; are you proud?" To which he replies, "Honey, I couldn't be happier than if they were based on real grades!"

All this demonstrates just how problematic grading is; it is an imprecise science, yet one on which society places great emphasis. In my experience, it is always best for the Headteacher to support the professional judgement of the teachers, encourage them to predict the grade they *genuinely* think the pupil will achieve, and then not to negotiate. Negotiated predictions nearly always lead to problems on results day.

## Using IQ testing

The term 'IQ' is old-fashioned and has gone out of use because the idea of an 'intelligence quotient' implies that a person is entirely limited by the intelligence they were born with. The term educators use now is 'cognitive ability', and – to all intents and purposes – it means the same thing! There are a number of commercial companies who offer banks of tests for pupils of various ages which are used as general predictors of academic attainment. Behind those predictors lie millions of pieces of historic data which have been collated by academics to show the colouration between the cognitive ability test scores and the GCSE grades achieved. The tests are 'standardised', which means that a score of 100 represents the average of UK pupils. The top of the scale is 140 and the bottom around 60. Generally speaking, pupils with scores averaging lower than 85 tend to need additional learning support. Typically, the tests cover the following three areas of cognitive ability:

- Verbal reasoning (VR), which tests the pupil's vocabulary and understanding of concepts.
- Non-verbal reasoning (NVR), which tests the pupil's ability to use logic and also to persevere – the obvious answer is often not the right answer.
- Quantitative (Q) ability, which is essentially a test of numerical skills.

The temptation is to take the three scores (VR, NVR, and Q) and average them to produce one overall cognitive ability score, but caution is needed here. An average score of 105 might be achieved with three scores all very close to 105 but equally could be achieved but one score of 105, one of 70, and one of 140. If the school relies on the average of the three scores, it can potentially mask some extreme strengths and weaknesses.

These tests can be very useful, but the results need to be interpreted by someone experienced. For instance, a strong VR score coupled with a much weaker NVR score may demonstrate why a pupil can appear to be very articulate but also unable to put ideas together to create a complete understanding of a concept. Strong NVR and Q scores coupled with a relatively weak VR score might lead a pupil to perform disappointingly in public exams. Given that nearly all public exams use the medium of language, a pupil with this profile could benefit hugely from extra support to strengthen their verbal reasoning.

## Who needs to know the test scores

It can be useful, when staff are discussing pupils, for the most recent test scores to be read out. That will provide an opportunity for teachers to realign their impressions of a pupil with what the statistical predictions are saying. So teachers need to know the scores, but otherwise, they should mostly be kept confidential, meaning that they should not be recorded on digital or paper registers which might be casually overlooked by a pupil. The dangers of telling pupils their scores are a) the scores are not particularly accurate, especially at predicting public exam results in subjects like PE, music or art, and b) we don't want to damage their inherent motivation to work hard. If a pupil is told their scores and predictions are high, they may misinterpret that as meaning their natural intelligence will get them the best grades without them needing to study. Conversely, a pupil who is made aware of low scores and expectations may despair and give up.

It can be argued that parents have a right to know the scores and should be told. However, caution must be taken in delivering this information. My practice was not to make a big deal about these test scores, and I certainly didn't add them to pupils' written reports. But if a parent showed a genuine interest, I would make time to sit down with them, face to face, to explain carefully and thoroughly what the scores were, how they had been generated, and how best to interpret them.

## Added value

Cognitive ability scores are a useful tool to inform teachers about performance and potential. They can also be used to generate 'value-added' scores. This is where the predictions of performance in public exams made one, two, or three years before the exam year are matched against what is actually achieved in those exams. If a pupil outperforms the prediction, then the school can be said to have 'added value' to that pupil.

As things stand, the government measure of value added in secondary schools is based on scores achieved by pupils at the end of Key Stage 2 SATs exams – the validity of which statisticians and teachers constantly question. The measures are further complicated by taking into account only specific GCSE subjects taken in particular combinations, resulting in a score called 'Progress 8'. Progress 8 is arcane and unnecessarily complex to the extent that the public and the media largely ignore it, whereas value-added scores based on cognitive ability testing tend to be more accurate and a lot easier to explain and understand.

## Summary

How to use assessment in the most effective ways – and how to generate data that is accurate enough to reveal strengths and weaknesses – are contested areas of leadership. The Headteacher new in post will be influenced by both the practice they helped administer in their previous setting and the practice they inherit at the new school. Some teachers will be very familiar with particular systems and may resist change. Whatever system the Headteacher adopts, and however they calibrate the importance of data, it is vital that their rationale is well thought through and that it aligns with their vision and values.

## Notes

1 Dylan Wiliam and Paul Black, *Inside the Black Box: Raising Standards Through Classroom Assessment*. Pub Kings College, London, 1998.
2 *Clueless*. Paramount Pictures, 1995.

# 24 Appraisal

It is hard to imagine a school where appraisals are not an important, formal moment to support the work of employees. The implementation of a system can be tricky, mostly because it takes up a lot of time and because creating genuine consistency across the team of appraisers is nearly impossible. Appraisals may cause employees to be cynical, scornful, or even fearful - but they need to be done and done well.

Appraisals usually include a formal element of lesson observation. Observing a lesson is not a neutral act. This is what Tom Sherrington,[1] a former Headteacher and now influential thought leader in education, writes about lesson observations:

> Teacher thinks: "Don't you dare walk into my classroom for 10-20 minutes, with all your status and biases, and then presume to write to me or to just tell me what I could have done better! Like you just 'know'. Talk to me first; ask me about my view of it and let's discuss some solutions to some of the inherent challenges this demanding work presents. If you can help me, that's great; if all you can do is judge - you're not welcome."

His point - that lesson observations can feel like something that is done to a teacher rather than something that results in co-created suggestions for development - is well made.

## It's all in the design

The way a Headteacher designs the appraisal system will say a lot about their ideas about how to get the best from the school's employees. Though far less common now, some appraisal processes are even linked to pay, meaning that appraisal becomes high stakes and stressful. Here are some guidelines which lead to an appraisal system which helps motivate employees and is not overbearing or overburdensome for managers:

1. An appraisal interview is not the time to deliver warnings about poor performance or put in place competency procedures. That can be awkward if the employee is indeed performing poorly at the time regular appraisal comes round, but nonetheless, this guidance must be followed.
2. Leaders need first to decide on the length of the appraisal cycle - usually either once a year, or once every two years. If an annual cycle is chosen, thought needs to be given to time and human resources, because appraisal should not be rushed. The most appropriate appraiser needs to be allocated to each employee. The overall management of the scheme needs to be realistically achievable.
3. Appraisal should begin with a document sent to the employee describing the process clearly and precisely so that expectations on both sides are clear. This document needs to make transparent the purpose of appraisal - that it is a **formal** moment for the school and employee to work together to review performance and discuss positive adjustments that might be made.
4. Inviting the appraisee to complete a simple questionnaire is a good starting point for discussion at the interview. Those questions could be the following:

    a. What has gone well for you at work since the last appraisal or since you started working here?
    b. What has not gone so well for you at work since the last appraisal or since you started working here?
    c. In what ways do you think the school could enhance your working life, e.g. training, time allocation?
    d. Is there anything you would like to add at this point?

The questionnaire needs to be returned to the appraiser at least 24 hours before the diarised appraisal interview.

5. If a teacher (or any employee with direct contact with pupils in a teaching and learning capacity) is being appraised, then an observation should be arranged. The appraiser may stipulate the lesson to be observed or may want to chat through the suitability of a lesson by agreement. Prior to the lesson observation, some planning should be submitted. This need not be exhaustive, or a significant departure from normal practice, but the appraiser needs to understand the *context* of the lesson being observed – what has gone before and what the learning expectation might be. In addition, the appraiser should ask for information about how the needs of SEND pupils are being met in the lesson so that this can be assessed too. Having guidelines (rather than a template) for what should generally be included in a lesson plan can avoid things going wrong at both appraisal and inspection. The lesson plan, along with the questionnaire, should be submitted 24 hours before the appraisal interview.

6. The lesson observation takes place. The appraiser should do all in their power to make the employee feel at ease, and that might mean being tucked away at the back of the classroom with head down, or the opposite – being very present and joining in. To save time, the appraiser might spend part of the observation making notes on the employee's questionnaire and lesson plan. Notes taken relating to the lesson itself should be written in a form which doesn't need a lot of re-working so that the appraisal report is, in effect, being part written as the lesson is being observed.

7. The interview needs to take place as soon after the lesson observation as possible so that what happened is fresh in the minds of both the employee and the appraiser. The interview should start with the lesson observation and the discussion needs to aim for some co-created ideas about how to improve. If negative comments need to be made, then couching them as questions can be a good way to bring the employee into the discussion. For example, "I notice you had some of the SEND pupils at the back of the room; do you think their engagement might be better if they were sat further forward?" That example is a good one because it not only helps the appraiser avoid being didactic, it also allows for the real possibility that the teacher placed those pupils there for good reasons. In this way, the interview moves towards some agreed **'areas for consideration'** – not 'targets' or 'action points'. This enhances professional accountability and motivation, rather than leaving the appraisee feeling patronised and preached at.

8. The appraisal report is written up by the appraiser as a draft as quickly as possible to maintain momentum. The draft report is sent to the appraisee with a strict response

time. Adjustments may be suggested for consideration but must be made quickly; otherwise, the report will become irrelevant. If no comments or suggested amendments are made, the appraiser is invited to sign the report and it is put on their file; it then forms part of their formal performance record.

## Learning walks

Learning walks can be very useful, too, but they don't produce the same overview of a teacher as a formal observation. Each technique has its place and learning walks are a useful way to gain a snapshot of how things are going in a classroom when a senior leader drops by. To be fair to teachers, it is appropriate to notify them that learning walks will be taking place during a given period, just so they are not wrong-footed by the appearance of a senior leader at the door. Some teachers can become very anxious when observed, and senior leaders should be sensitive to this.

## Appraising non-teaching staff

Except for the lesson observation, most of the guidelines in this chapter apply to non-teaching staff as well. Should the appraiser formally watch the grounds staff mow the field? Probably not, though some incidental observations of their work may form part of the feedback at the appraisal interview. For example, the appraiser may have noticed that the ground staff member rarely wears waterproof clothing and gets soaked when it rains. The school may question why this is and offer to provide suitable attire.

## 360° Appraisals

For senior leaders – members of the school community with significant line management responsibility – 360° reviews are sometimes performed. This entails garnering the views of a cross-section of the people that particular leader encounters. That list will include not just co-selected members of the team they line manage, but also the people who line manage them or to whom they report – including people from the Top Layer. Care needs to be taken to ensure that the appraisee is happy with the process, because this can quickly come to be seen as a witch hunt if it is revealed that things are not going well.

## Note

1  Teacherhead.com

# 25 Finding balance and managing staff

It can be argued that if the Head is having a bad day, then everyone is having a bad day.

That's especially true of staff because they are the ones, out of the four estates, who look most to the Head for leadership. In this chapter, we will look at how the school's leadership can use the staff as a resource to support their own sense of balance and wellbeing. Having a happy and supportive staff room is one of the most significant drivers in finding and sustaining balance for the Headteacher.

Some leaders, in any walk of life, feel that they don't need to be liked in order to the job well. The leader has to make tough decisions, and that is inevitably going to make some people dislike them, some of the time. But that doesn't justify leadership behaviour that engenders dislike by most people for most of the time!

Being liked makes the job a lot easier. If the Headteacher is liked, then

- Tough decisions, like compulsory redundancies or changes in pay and conditions, are easier to manage.
- People will be nice to you, share a joke, make sure you're okay, welcome you into their world. All that helps with balance.
- You won't need to be lonely.
- When times are tough and you're having to deal with conflict, at least you won't dread walking into the staff room.
- Staff will be motivated simply by the fact that you are kind, compassionate and empathetic.

That also means that **likability** is an important quality in all school leaders.

Being liked equates with being trusted and if people trust the Head, then decisions can be made without lengthy explanations and justification. Simply put, trust makes the business of running a school a lot smoother and easier.

## What are the ways the Headteacher can engender trust?

The reason we're asking this question in this chapter about Headteacher wellbeing and balance is because you reap what you sow. If staff trust the Headteacher, then that is a huge bonus, but the Headteacher needs to put the work in to gain that trust – especially in the early days as a new appointee.

So how do you build trusting relationships with staff?

- Create changes that make the daily experience of working at the school better. These need not be big or expensive gestures but can be simple things like providing snacks and free tea/coffee for break time, or a snack for those working late after the end of the school day.

DOI: 10.4324/9781003517825-28

- The Headteacher should be their **authentic self**. This is different from the idea of *authentic leadership*, which means ensuring that the values espoused by the Head are ones they live by themselves. In the context of building trust, being their authentic self means being unafraid to share some personal stuff. Conversations with the Headteacher, however casual, are constantly monitored, remembered, shared and commented on – often for many years. Even after the Head has left the school, you will hear people say things like "I remember that time when we were talking about sport and they said they always cried when watching the Olympics. That strikes me – I don't know why – but it showed they were human." Trust and likability come from being **relatable**. Relatability means staff are more likely to be empathetic when times are hard.
- With teaching staff, relatability is straightforward because the Headteacher is or was a teacher themselves. Therefore, engaging in conversations about the real and specific challenges of classroom practice really helps.
- With non-teaching staff, relatability is harder, partly because they are not usually in the staff room at break and lunchtimes. Alongside formal conversations, it is therefore important to share small talk, like asking about people's families, likes, and dislikes. Some Headteachers make a point of knowing the name and occupation of every staff member's partner or some other personal circumstances – for example, that they have moved in with their mother to help after their father died.
- The Headteacher can be open and straightforward about the strategic plans for the school. For example, the refurbishment of a classroom block has been announced, and a staff member casually asks how plans are progressing. It might feel a bit strange to give an update to this person rather than a formal announcement to everyone, but it's possible there's nothing significant to say that justifies a whole staff update. So the reply could simply be along the lines of "A meeting with the builders was held yesterday and it looks like we might need to go back to planning, but overall, we're still on course to complete on time." That staff member feels trusted that the Head shared those details and has been transparent. **Retentiveness is the enemy of relatability and is a barrier to building trust.**

## The more you give, the more you get

All of this sounds like more effort for the Headteacher – attending the staff room regularly and engaging in staff-wide conversations in which they must get to know everyone, be open and transparent about the school, and be prepared to open up about themselves to some extent, too – but it's worth it.

If the Head is feeling stressed, and reserves of niceness are running on fumes, then none of this seems feasible. But it is at those moments that the previous work in building trust is cashed in. The Head walks into the staff room intent on just pouring themselves a coffee and reading the trade papers without drawing attention to themselves. To others in the room, it's clear they're not their bouncy selves today and someone will take the initiative to cheer them up. They might offer something like,

"You know that new reading initiative we're piloting this term? I just have to tell you, it is already reaping fantastic results. Would you have time to pop into my classroom this afternoon and I can show you how it's going?"

Or

"I bumped into Josh Taylor at the weekend – you remember how tough things were for him in Year 7? Well, he's at Uni now and doing really well – he sends his love."

By building trust with staff, the Headteacher is recruiting a small army of supporters who will willingly provide help on both professional and personal levels when needed. The Headteacher needs to remember that, just as they and their leadership team observe and monitor the performance and wellbeing of the staff, so the staff are watching them, too. Staff *see* the Head, and if trust is there, they will invest in the Head finding balance as much as any other paid member of the school community.

## Difficult HR moments

When considering how experienced Headteachers might rank order the challenges of dealing with each of the four estates in a school, some will place managing staff as the most challenging, and others as the least. Wherever they are ranked, there is no doubt that dealing with an underperforming member of staff can be one of the most stressful aspects of running a school. In Chapter 15 – 'Leadership competencies', we looked at the process of terminating an employee's contract, but we did not acknowledge the professional and emotional strain it can place on the Headteacher.

Again, *everyone* is watching as the narrative of how a staff member is dismissed unfolds – and *everyone* will have a comment and an opinion. The focus such events draws from the community only adds to the stress experienced by the leader. Doubly important then to get it right, but the negative emotions that inevitably accompany these situations can get in the way. It is not uncommon for the departing staff member to turn on the Head with a personal attack and try to threaten and manipulate. There may well be moments when emotions such as anger, resentment and bitterness – accompanied by feelings of unfairness and abandonment – make self-control very hard for the Head. But any departure from the strict and relentless appearance of professionalism will make things worse.

The best mindset for these moments is one in which compassion, long-term vision, and objectivity reign supreme. Above all else, and however bad the Headteacher may feel about the circumstances of the departing employee, it is the welfare and quality of the pupils' education that justifies the actions that are being taken.

There were several times I had to dismiss people from the school. On one occasion, the newly dismissed employee's wife immediately decided to end their marriage – this being the final straw. Again, I had to remind myself that the needs of the pupils came first – that's the job.

# Part IV: Parents and partnership

# 26 Creating partnerships between parents and the school

This 'gloves off' chapter shines a light on the negative influence many parents have on the effective running of schools and suggests specific and positive strategies to change that situation. For far too long, teachers and Headteachers have taken the view that appeasing difficult parents is the best option. This has contributed to a fundamental lack of respect for educators on the part of many parents, which has de-skilled and disempowered the profession as a whole. The answer lies in a strict adherence to a partnership model, and a home-school contract which contains consequences and sanctions for parents who break that contract.

Whether parents are paying for their children's education directly through fees or indirectly through taxation, they are not the customers of the service being provided by the school. The customer is the child, because it is they who are in receipt of the service. Parents are therefore not customers but partners in the delivery of education, and their role is focused on 'upbringing' and 'raising', as opposed to the imparting of knowledge and understanding.

## Who's responsible?

There is a wonderful cartoon that has been around for a while. It depicts two scenes: one in the 1960s and one in the present day. In both scenes a pair of parents and their child are sitting in front of their child's teacher discussing progress. In the 1960s' version, one parent is saying to their *child*: "Your grades are down, so you are just going to need to work harder." In the present-day version, the parent is saying to the *teacher*: "His grades are down, so you're just going to need to work harder."

The relationship between parents and schools can become very conflictual; it is often characterised by aggressive and abusive communication from parents to the school, and usually vain attempts by the teachers to appease those parents. We need a plan to fix this.

The problem seems to be one of respect; the respect previous generations of parents had for teachers has drained away steadily over the last few decades. Respect has largely been replaced by demand and over-entitlement. Trust has been a casualty, too; most parents, even the supportive ones, don't fully trust schools to do the right thing by their children. They are quick to jump to negative conclusions, and many have no inhibition about choosing to attack the school. Attacks in some quarters of society take the form of verbal and physical threats, with parents standing in the school reception area shouting at the teacher or support worker, using threatening and highly intimidating language. In other quarters, this aggression is played out in the form of lawyers' letters and threats of legal action.

There are many reasons why this erosion of trust has happened, but one thing we can be sure of is that it is NOT because teachers care less than they used to, or that they are less professional or less accountable. The change has been in the attitudes and expectations of parents. Politicians have not helped, loading ever greater layers of accountability on schools not just through the inspection regime but through regulation

DOI: 10.4324/9781003517825-30

and safeguarding responsibilities as well. The network of children's services has been under-funded over many years to the extent that they can support only a tiny proportion of the families they were originally designed to serve. Because of these political decisions, teachers are now expected to be front-line social workers, mental health practitioners, police and nurses. Teachers have reluctantly accepted these additional roles partly because they care so passionately about the children in their schools, and partly because they feel they have no choice.

Reporting on the education system post-pandemic, mainstream media commentors pointed towards a collective sigh of parental relief as the baton passed back to schools to be the sole custodians of educational responsibility for their little ones. Yet a worrying number of parents now have expectations for teachers to be contactable 24/7.

Have we passed from a pandemic of COVID-19 to a pandemic of over-entitlement?

It is NOT okay for the parent of a 17-year-old girl to say to the Pastoral Care Deputy Head, "My daughter's friendships are going badly wrong, and I need you to fix that. You should know that she has an eating disorder, and if she slips into being an anorexic, I will hold you personally accountable."

An 8-year-old boy was unhappy when he was asked to walk down a path on a field trip side by side with his teacher rather than with a peer because there were an odd number of children. It is NOT okay for the parent of that child to accuse the teacher of "emotionally raping" her son.

Some parents feel it is appropriate to email at any time during the night, at weekends, or in the holidays. Their emails can be angry and offensive, written with little filter or regard for accuracy. Communication can be personal and undermining, apportioning blame without proper knowledge and demanding that other people's children are punished – and the emails keep coming, legions of them; each one has to be processed and dealt with calmly, professionally, and compassionately, no matter the tone of the original message.

The power dynamic between parents and teachers has become unbalanced, amounting to a situation where teachers across the nation are being bullied. The more teachers give of their time, energy and professionalism beyond teaching, the less they seem to be held in esteem. Like the classic victims of bullying, the more they try to appease, the worse and more frequent the onslaughts of abuse become.

## Time to fight back

Does 'fight back' sound pugnacious and inflammatory? I make no apology for that language. I have stood in front of many groups of teachers and seen the look on their faces when we start talking about the negative influence parental behaviours has on their lives, their emotional wellbeing, and their motivation to carry on in this profession. It's genuinely shocking. When the discussion begins to touch on what we might do to improve the relationship with parents, all I ever hear is strategies to appease – strategies to increase and improve the quality of communication with home, to write more bulletins, to hold more Parents' Evenings, to consult more, to include more. But it doesn't work, because this is an abusive relationship.

## Communication with home

In the interests of balance, I should say that being the recipient of school communication is not easy. One parent wrote to me pointing out that she had to scan across nine different communication channels to be sure she understood what was happening for her child. I hadn't realised just how far the proliferation had gone, and it was quite some task, working with my Communications Officer, to reduce the channels down to something manageable. We cleaned up our act, and I was grateful to that parent for her constructive criticism. The digitalisation of home communication has been helpful in some ways, but it's far from simple. As much as anything, the technology keeps changing, even decades after email became a thing. So schools roll out a new shiny digital platform which will serve all the needs of all the people, only to find it superseded within a matter of months. And it's no good 'sticking with what we all know', because the new version is genuinely better!

## How do we fight back?

Okay, that's enough of the counter argument. Let's talk strategy; let's get down to the nitty-gritty – how can we make this better?

What does a healthy relationship between school and home look like?

- Partnership, as in a shared responsibility for children that is clearly defined for both parties.
- Trust so that parents don't automatically assume the worst, that their child is being overlooked and nobody cares.
- Courteous and constructive communication – *always*.

## Partnership

There's nothing new about this idea, but schools seem to have lost sight of the obvious fact that the very best way to support children is for the school and parents to work together, in partnership. The partnership concept has been hijacked by a power imbalance and a fundamental dispute over *ownership*. I have noticed, when involved in a conversation with a parent that is not going well, that the parent will start to use the words 'my son' or 'my daughter'. This possessive expression, for me, is a passive-aggressive move in which the parent is claiming superior knowledge of and sovereignty over the child in question. The use of this terminology fundamentality erodes the sense that adults are working together.

## The dentist analogy

Look at it this way: when a parent takes their child to the dentist, there is a very particular dynamic. If the dentist finds decaying teeth, they will explain to the *child* the need for twice-daily careful brushing and the benefits of reducing sugar intake. But the dentist isn't really talking to the child; they are talking to the parent, because all three people in that situation – dentist, child, parent – know that the tooth decay is down (to some extent, at least) to the inability of the parent to ensure healthy dental care. This is a partnership. The parent's duty is to impart the value system, both intellectual and practical, that will ensure the child adopts the right habits. The child's role is to listen, learn, action, and embed those habits. The dentist's role is to impart wisdom, knowledge, and understanding and to monitor and report on progress to both child and parent. Sounds like the ideal model for a home-school agreement to me!

Teachers need to be more dentist, and while we're talking in medical metaphors, schools need to be more like a **doctor's surgery**. Patients cannot and do not expect to be able to communicate directly with their doctor, whether that is a general practitioner (GP) or a surgeon. All communication has to pass through receptionists and administrators. There is no reason why schools should not adopt the same approach: meetings by appointment only, emails and messages sent exclusively to a central address which is monitored by a dedicated communications team. Contact between school and parent is entirely controlled by the school: senior leaders, teachers, and support workers are protected from abuse and get on with the job, free from bullying.

## Setting boundaries

For the partnership between home and school to work effectively, there need to be clear expectations and boundaries. We can achieve these in three ways:

1. Setting out **expectations** through the information given on application. When a parent applies to a school, there needs to be a document and/or video – which is compulsory to engage with – which sets out the expectations that the school has of the parents. This information will make excellent material for Headteacher speeches at Open Days. The information needs to stress very firmly how important it is that the partnership is adhered to for the wellbeing, success, and happiness of the child. The delivery should be self-confident and assertive without being pompous or condescending. The impression needs to be of a school that has high self-esteem and values its own worth as a place of education serving its community. This information leads to the home-school agreement.
2. **Home-school agreement.** Lawyers tell me you can never make this agreement legally binding, but that doesn't mean that the document should not feel deliberate and serious. For instance, the school should refuse entry until the agreement is signed by all relevant caregivers in the home. The signatories will be given a copy, and another copy will be kept on file for reference. New caregivers should sign the agreement, even if the child has been at the school for some time. Most importantly, this is a document where a parent should tick the box "I have read the terms and conditions" only after they have *actually read* the terms and conditions. Maintenance and consistency over the administration of this is crucial; this can't be a "We did this for a couple of years, but now it's slipped" kind of thing.
3. **Communication.** Perhaps the most important aspect of the home-school agreement is the directive that all communication between school employees and parents must **always** and **without exception** be courteous and constructive. That is, after all, the minimum standard any teacher in the world works by. It's about levelling the playing field.

*Creating partnerships between parents and the school* 113

It's not fair for a parent to shout at and abuse a teacher. Teachers feel like they are the proverbial 'sitting ducks' or the 'fish in the barrel' being shot at.

## Consistency

Having got this far, the next and perhaps harder hurdle is implementation. What happens when the home-school agreement is broken? Here's a stab at what the 'sanctions' part of the agreement might look like:

> The signatories of this agreement acknowledge that there may be times when the school and parental signatories do not agree on the best way forward for [name of child]. Examples may include the use of the school's sanctions policy in relation to poor standards of behaviour by [name of child] and/or other children. Disputes may arise from teachers' assessments and reports or reported instances of conflict arising between members of the community.
>
> In all instances, communication must be courteous and constructive. This is a vital and a central part of this agreement and there can be no exceptions to this rule. If an employee of the school fails to adhere to this rule, they can expect to be sanctioned in relation to the terms of their employment. If a parent signatory does not communicate courteously and constructively (in all forms, verbal and written) then they can expect the school to respond appropriately. The school's response may range from requesting an apology, through to a complete and comprehensive ban on all communication with the school (in any form) and exclusion from the school premises. The school will always demand the highest standards of communication from every parental signatory in every instance. This will strengthen the partnership and benefit [name of child]. This rule applies equally to extended family members or close family friends who are acting on behalf of the parent signatories in their communications with the school.
>
> Parents may choose to make a complaint, and no part of this agreement inhibits their right to do so. However, this agreement does cover the language and tone used in a complaint. The fact that a complaint is being made does not exempt the parental signatories from the terms of this agreement which govern the tone of all communications as described above.

And then push back. Push back against the shouty abuse; push back against the vexatious lawyer's letter. Don't take it lying down; stop appeasing. Remember, every time you appease, you're making things worse for the child.

# 27 Dealing with complaints

Dealing with complaints in the education sector is a highly evolved part of regulation and compliance. There is a set way to deal with complaints laid down in the Complaints Policy which in turn is defined strictly by regulation. This is a zero-sum game, and the only thing a Headteacher should focus on is not getting it wrong!

## Being compliant

The Complaints Policy, which must be published on the school's website and be available in print, will lay out the precise way in which complaints will be dealt with. Ironically, the easiest thing to get wrong is not following the policy to the letter – errors to do with recording are particularly common.

All correspondence relating to a complaint needs to be archived, and particular attention needs to be given to the advice in Chapter 15 – 'Leadership competencies' about GDPR and internal communication relating to the complaint. It can be useful to have a physical folder for complaints which might include a narrative from the Head, alongside all the other correspondence, once the complaint is resolved. That correspondence will need to include contemporaneous notes taken of phone calls and meetings with parents and staff.

The complaint is not regarded as concluded until a note is added to the file to that effect. This is an easy oversight to make, since the conclusion may well be signalled by the lack of a response from the complainer. If that is the case, then the file note should say, "It is now x weeks since the school has heard from Mr and Mrs X, and the school now reasonably regards the complaint as resolved."

Stage 3 of a complaint requires a panel hearing to be convened. It is at this point that some fresh minds need to get involved, and one of those fresh minds must be someone external to both the school and the complainer. Someone who fits this category is not easy to find, so consideration is needed to using local contacts who might be suitable. It is also important that someone from the Top Layer, who hasn't been directly involved in the meetings and correspondence so far, is in attendance.

Don't forget to inform the school's insurers if there is the remotest possibility that the school may be held liable following the complaint. That would include any complaint from a parent that related to health and safety or employment rights from an employee.

The school is fully entitled to regard a gripe as just that – an irritation rather than a complaint – and it might be that the Complaints Policy requires the complainer to make it clear that they are lodging a formal complaint by using those specific words.

Finally, the Complaints Policy must contain information about how many complaints were received by the school in the previous year. Generally speaking, that refers to Stage 2 complaints where the Headteacher or Chair of Governors has made a formal response or, of course, Stage 3 complaints. How honest schools are about this is questionable – when I see a school claiming no complaints in the previous year, I always wonder how they have decided to categorise their complaints!

## Dealing with the complaint

We have looked at the compliance side of this; now let's examine the best way to 'deal' with complaints. Given that I have argued forcefully against the idea of appeasing parents, you might expect me to be advising a fairly robust response to parental complaints – but not so.

In resolving a complaint, the school wants the following:

- the complainer to feel fairly dealt with, heard, and vindicated – if possible
- to learn from the complaint and amend policy and practice – if appropriate
- for no complaints of a similar nature to recur

To achieve these outcomes, correspondence needs to be carefully thought through, drafted, and checked for meaning and sense. Every word will be pored over and used as evidence if the complaint ultimately ends up in the hands of lawyers. In Stage 1, where an informal resolution is sought, the language used needs to be no less formal than if the Headteacher was writing a witness statement for court.

If the Headteacher is in a position to take the complaint on the chin and apologise, then that is probably the best course of action. The intention is always to avoid escalation whilst not setting precedents which will make things more awkward in the future. So, along with the explanation for what went wrong, consider including the words "I apologise on behalf of the school – this should not have happened and I have taken steps to ensure it doesn't happen again."

For example, let's take an email from a parent that is couched in quite dramatic terms, such as:

> My son has just come home and tells me that he had nothing to eat at lunchtime because there was literally nothing he could stomach. I can't believe that I am paying for a service from the school that is so poor that my son has to go hungry. I would like this complaint noted and a refund for today's lunch. I look forward to hearing from you soon. I trust that there will be suitable food for him to eat tomorrow and that this situation will not be repeated.

On investigation, it turns out that the boy in question was unreasonably late to lunch, arriving a full five minutes after everyone else. His lateness was his choice. Though his favoured food had run out, there were still two other dishes on offer, plus vegetables. Staff report that they have seen him eat the same dishes that were on offer that day on other occasions, so the school knows that the boy *chose* to refuse the food rather than the food being unpalatable for him specifically.

It is tempting to apportion at least some of the blame to the boy, but that is not necessarily going to resolve the complaint. If anything, it is likely to inflame the situation, leading the parent to take the complaint to Stage 2. There is no advantage in allowing that to happen. Instead, the return email might read as follows:

> Dear Mrs [ _____ ],
>
> I acknowledge your complaint of yesterday's date. I have now had a chance to look into what happened. I apologise on behalf of the school that your son went hungry yesterday; that is disappointing and should not have happened. I have taken steps to ensure it doesn't happen again.
>
> Yours,
> Headteacher

The "steps" the Headteacher then takes to "ensure it doesn't happen again" are to emphasise to the *boy* that he needs to get to lunch on time, to suggest that there *were* viable options for him to eat that day, and to encourage him to talk to the Headteacher, if this situation should ever arise again, before going home to complain.

I like this example because it is common for complaints to arise from a story being told by a pupil at home. Parents can only react to what they are told, and they may have no reason to suspect the story is only partially true. The way to resolve these situations is to communicate with the parent in such a way as not to impugn the honesty of their child or humiliate them but to allow them to feel their complaint has landed so that they can retain their dignity. Meanwhile, the school works *with* and *through* the pupil, making it clear they understand that the story the pupil told at home was incomplete without actually accusing them of lying. If ever there was a child-centred way to run school, this is it!

## Some other common complaints

Through my work training teachers to become practitioners of the *Girls on Board* approach, I know that girls falling out through social media is very common. I acknowledge, of course, that boys fall out, too, and that the issue of boys' interaction with social media platforms can be very problematic, as well, but this example is about girls. Complaints relating to girls' fallouts pour into schools in extraordinary numbers. In incidental surveys I have conducted on LinkedIn, many teachers report receiving complaints about girls' friendship turbulence several times *a week*. The complaints follow similar patterns: the conflict has arisen during weekends or evenings, they include abusive texts or image generation, people are offended and hurt – *and* it's the school's job, apparently, to sort it all out.

These complaints cause teachers and pastoral care staff to spend many hours investigating and probing for the truth – time which is usually wasted. The truth becomes tangled; texts are deleted, redacted, or happened on Snapchat, in which case they vanished after ten seconds.

I want to propose a radical solution here – and please feel to reproduce the following in your response to these types of complaints. What if . . . instead of investigating and regarding these situations as somehow in the purview of the school, the Head of Year replies in the following manner:

Dear [ _____ ],

It has come to the school's attention that your daughter has recently been involved in exchanges of messages and posts on social media platforms which have resulted in conflict arising amongst the girls in her year group.

This email does not seek to apportion blame in any way, but we wish to point out that these messages and posts were sent in the evenings and during the weekends on devices owned by you, on an internet service which you pay for and while your daughter was under your supervision.

We would be grateful if you could monitor and regulate your daughter's use of social media platforms more robustly to avoid further conflict arising in the future.

Yours,
Head of Year

As I wrote in Chapter 26, it's time to push back. Indeed, if you ask the girls themselves (which I have many times) whether things get better or worse when the grown-ups get involved in their friendship turbulence, they will tell you, without hesitation, that things get worse.

These situations often lead to complaints of bullying. As we saw in Chapter 10, all accusations have to be investigated, but the vast majority of bullying complaints are found to be groundless which, again, consumes huge amounts of time. Convincing parents of the dangers of 'crying wolf' is not easy, but the following is an attempt:

Dear [ _____ ],

I confirm that I have received your recent communication in which you claim your daughter is being bullied. You helpfully relayed the story behind this accusation and the names of the accused, as well.

The school always takes seriously and investigates any reports of bullying, and that is what we have done. It is our policy to operate a triage system to inform our investigation and that involves working carefully through the two key markers of what bullying looks like if it is happening. If the triage reveals that the key markers of bullying are missing, then no further investigation is undertaken.

In triaging the story you told us about, the school has investigated whether there is

- a serious imbalance of power between your daughter and the accused.
- evidence of intentional acts of violence, destruction of property, or extreme and prolonged exclusionary behaviour affecting your daughter and/or others.

Our investigation revealed that there has been conflict between the girls in your daughter's year group and that she has been involved in and affected by this conflict. The conflict we have become aware of has involved a level of relational aggression on all sides. We have therefore concluded that, since there is no serious imbalance of power and there have been no intentional acts of violence, destruction of property, or extreme and prolonged exclusionary behaviour, this situation should not be classified as bullying.

However, a number of girls have been distressed by the conflict that has arisen, and we will bring the girls together in school very soon to resolve the turbulence and empower them to restore harmony in their relationships.

I would encourage you, should you be concerned about your daughter's experience of school in the future, to consult with the Head of Year first before concluding that an accusation of bullying is appropriate. Every pupil has their own perception of what has been happening to them, and those perceptions need to be analysed and curated before time is spent on investigations.

Yours,
The Headteacher

## Vexatious complaints

The Department for Education publishes a guide[1] for complaints and complaints policies. At the end of the guide, there are several pages dedicated to defining vexatious, serial, or persistent complaints and what to do in response. It *is* in the power of the school to ban or severely restrict communication and points of contact and also to ban parents from school premises. In my view, the Headteacher should not hesitate to act in accordance with this guidance where appropriate.

## Note

1  Gov.uk, *Best Practice Guidance for School Complaints Procedures*, 2020.

# 28 Reporting to parents

## Parents' Evenings

Research[1] in 2017 found that progress scores of children whose parents attended Parents' Evenings were distinctly better. On the other hand, Lepkowska and Nightingale in *Meet the Parents*[2] point at the **quality of conversations** between the teacher and parent as far more significant than whether the parents merely attend.

Providing teachers with a **framework** for parent consultations will improve the effectiveness of communication and build trust. Here are some ideas about how that framework can be designed.

Teachers should avoid jargon and quoting too much data; comparisons with the rest of the class are meaningless and need to be replaced by an understanding of placing each child within their own context of *what has gone before* and *where are we heading at this rate*. Sharing classwork can be useful, giving examples of strengths and weakness, if appropriate.

In particular, teachers need to be aware of the potential emotional impact on a parent when reporting on their child. Whatever the news – good, bad or indifferent – the parents' understanding of their child will be altered. Similarly, the news of a child's progress and the way it is delivered will have an impact on the parents' view of that teacher and how much they trust them. Telling a parent that their child is "No problem, they're doing fine" is frustrating. The parent might want to retort:

> Yes, I know she's no problem. That will be because she is the best human being that ever walked the earth. Now, I want you to tell me how she is going to fulfil her potential, because we need to be ambitious for her.

In defence of teachers, the back-to-back nature of parent consultations can be exhausting, and the worst moment can be when a parent sits before you and you can't remember who they are. To get around that problem, a simple and effective way is to require all parents to pick up a sticky name label at the door as they arrive. This serves both as a register of which parents have attended and to help teachers identify them. Unclaimed labels belong to the non-attenders.

Delivering some mini-training and reminders to teachers before each Parents' Evening can help things go smoothly. It is important for staff to remember that there are, essentially, two elements to reporting to parents: they need to know about **attainment and progress**, and they need to know about **engagement**.

## Reporting on attainment and progress

Reporting on attainment and progress can be tricky, because a pupil's current performance might be well below their potential. Informing the parent of that can prompt a shocked response, and they will be tempted to blame the teacher and/or school. It's therefore important, when reporting on attainment which is below expectation, for the teacher to be able to tell the parent immediately what strategies are being deployed to get the pupil back on track.

"I am not entirely happy with how things are going for your child so this is what we're going to do . . ." There is no gap between the negative report and the proposed solution.

## Reporting on engagement

While some parents will be interested in the data and what it shows, many prefer to hear about how their child is **enjoying** lessons. This is especially true in years where public exams are not the main focus. The teacher is less likely to have hard data on *enjoyment* and will need to rely on their memory of that individual child in their lessons. Teachers do well to have specific examples of good engagement to relay to parents – recording them as they happen or soon after. There is power in relaying specific moments, such as "I was delighted in the art lesson last week when your child asked me to explain perspective to him. He showed real persistence at that moment, because it had been clear he hadn't quite got it yet."

Parents also need to know whether their child is **happy**, has friends, and generally enjoys school life. That is where the form tutor comes in, or perhaps a member of the pastoral care team. Some form of information sharing between teachers prior to the Parents' Evening is therefore vital. That can be done via email, a notice on the staff room notice board, a Google form, or – my preference – a meeting. Perhaps a mixture of these forums works best, because it is not easy to discuss every child in the year group in a one-hour meeting. Meeting time is reserved for discussion of key pupils – e.g. pupils with SEND and pupils making significant progress or lack of progress. These meetings are also a chance for any teacher to ask, "Is it just me, or is child X showing signs of genius/neglect/coasting?" When others chime in, which they often do, we all now know more about that child who might otherwise have gone under the radar.

What is also useful in these pre-Parents' Evening meetings is for someone, perhaps a Head of Year, to read out the cognitive ability scores of any pupil that is being talked about. This not only refreshes everyone's memory about the profile of that pupil but also informs the subsequent discussion.

## Head's role

It depends on the size of the school as to what the nature of the Head's involvement is likely to be. The Head's role – if nothing else – can be simply be presence there in the hall, foyer, or corridors, picking up on little moments of joy and/or conflict. The Head is largely there in case a parent wants to discuss something further or take advice about wider educational issues. In my experience, parents rarely availed themselves of that opportunity, which I took as a good sign, though not a sign that my attendance wasn't still needed and useful. Presence can be everything, even if it is just the Head's face in the audience, at the back of the room, or at the door. In large schools, that role may need to be delegated to give the Head some relief.

We can, of course, use technology to host Parents' Evening, and various commercial digital platforms sprung up during the pandemic to facilitate this. Despite the rather brutal way in which calls are ended by the software, I found the strict time limit focused my thinking about the questions I wanted to ask parents and the comments I needed to make.

Some parents are keen to engage in these meetings but request alternative times. It feels churlish to deny them the chance to talk outside the scheduled Parents' Evening, but if everyone asked for this special treatment, the system would become untenable. There is no harm in complying with the request, but some reservations need to be expressed about how difficult it is going to be to arrange.

There should be no surprises or shocks when reporting in a Parents' Evening. If a serious message about performance or behaviour needs to be delivered, it should be done beforehand. Teachers should be advised that if they need to have an unavoidably challenging conversation with a parent at a Parents' Evening, they should inform a member of SLT who is attending so that they can pick up the pieces if necessary.

## Written reports

Schools will often adopt two versions of written reports – 'full written', and 'interim' or 'progress' reports. Both versions need reviewing and updating every two or three years. That is a reasonable expectation.

**Full written reports** use curriculum descriptors, teachers' comments and attainment grades. Some schools include progress grades, and those whose senior leaders have not yet read Wiliam and Black include effort grades.

The biggest struggle in getting full written reports as good as they can be is supporting teachers to write comments that are meaningful, accurate, grammatical, free from proofing errors, and spelt correctly. In bigger schools, a team dedicated to proofreading is needed, but – accuracy aside – the biggest challenge is getting teachers to write sentences that make sense, aren't too long, and make a useful remark.

To get around these recurring problems, I occasionally kept a spreadsheet on which I recorded how many mistakes each teacher made in a set of reports and the nature of those mistakes. That list included general spelling, incorrect spelling of pupil's name, incorrect pupil's name (I know, right?!), poor grammar, random double spaces between words, confusion about whether to use a comma after the word 'however', overlong sentences, repeated sentences, ranting, missing words, confusion between addressing the pupil and the parent, and lazy repetition of generalised remarks that could apply – and were applied – to every pupil. I would then publish the scores on the staff room notice board.

As with reporting to parents face to face, the teacher can never really know the state of mind of the audience as they receive the report on their child. Therefore, to avoid making crass errors of tone, I instructed all teachers to write their reports imagining that the parent audience was already furious, frustrated, and itching for a chance to complain. That ensured that every report on every child found something positive to say and delivered guidance for improvement gently and politely.

**Interim reports** are a quick 'at-a-glance' summary of data indicating progress, sometimes containing a comment from the form teacher or Head of Year. There are as many designs for this as there are schools. One effective format is to adopt a traffic light system against criteria agreed with staff. Those criteria might be things like the following:

- on course to achieve potential
- making progress
- attitudes to learning

- respect shown in the classroom
- completion of homework
- focus in class

The criteria listed in the interim report reflect what the school thinks are the most important focus for the partnership of school, parents, and pupils. This may seem obvious, but I have seen reports which just said, "Position in class," "Marks achieved," and "Class average marks achieved." It seems to me that that data set tells the parents nothing meaningful at all.

## Summary

As we have seen, there are many versions of reporting to parents, and getting it right is very dependent on the context of the school. In terms of establishing a trusting partnership between parents and school, the reporting system can play a significant role.

## Notes

1 Published by the Social Market Foundation and conducted by the Commission on Inequality in Education, 2017.
2 Dorothy Lepkowska and Julie Nightingale, *Meet the Parents*. Pub Routledge, 2019.

# 29 Working with the Parent-Teacher Association

Nearly all schools have a Parent-Teacher Association (PTA), though increasingly the teacher involvement is less and these associations are being re-branded as 'Friends of . . . School/Academy' with exclusively parent membership.

The main functions of the PTA are to raise money and to promote togetherness amongst the school community by organising events which are fun and popular. The two functions should ideally go hand in hand, though sometimes the committee will prioritise community cohesion above fund raising in order to ease the financial pressure of organising events and ensure there is no barrier to attendance.

## Allocating funds

How the PTA funds are spent can be controversial. Some PTAs will encourage staff to submit requests; others will have their own projects in mind. Staff going directly to the PTA to ask for funding without prior permission from the Headteacher can cause problems. For example, a teacher might request money for new costumes for the school play. The PTA might question why these funds can't be found from within the class or drama budget, given that the play happens every year. In fact, any request from staff can fall foul of the same question: "Why isn't the school funding this anyway?" That's why involvement of the Headteacher is needed, even if it is just to filter, justify, and recommend the requests.

Finding suitable areas for funding is surprisingly hard because the most exciting projects are ones which feel like a 'bonus'. It is most appealing if the funding is going towards something that feels like an 'extra' and not just catching up. For example, funding a new IT server just feels like the school has failed to budget for obsolescence and replacement costs. A common favourite project is focused on the playground, providing additional toys, climbing frames, and benches.[1] Concrete table tennis tables are a good example – the school would be hard pushed to justify such expenditure, but they make an excellent addition to the facilities.

## The committee

The effectiveness of the PTA is often almost entirely dependent on the people who run the committee – and that sometimes is just one person. That means that the vision and values that guide the work of the PTA tend to change with every shift in personnel.

## Headteacher's role

A new Headteacher will surely want to attend at least the first PTA meeting on arrival and encourage the committee in their work. After that, it's a judgement call whether to attend or not. It may be necessary for the Headteacher to usher in a new era – re-imagining the 'PTA' as 'Friends of . . . ' and therefore releasing the obligation on teachers to attend.

There can be a tendency for PTA committees to fall into reminiscing and nostalgic rumination, which can be unhelpful and enervating. The Headteacher can provide an ethical framework which can help the committee to see everything they do as useful, positive, and worthwhile. There is a natural ebb and flow of interest in PTA events, and perhaps the most useful contribution the Headteacher can make is to reassure the committee that these things happen, and postmortems are unhelpful and quite depressing. Long, nostalgic discussions can turn into moaning sessions which in turn put off new members and new ideas.

Equally, the Headteacher is there to release the committee from traditions which have passed their time without necessarily having to examine why. For example, the PTA traditionally provides refreshments during the interval of the school play, but it is becoming increasingly hard to recruit parents to help and there is always an issue about being thanked. A parent might become disillusioned because the PTA was not mentioned in the programme – an oversight of the new teacher in charge of drama, but which has caused offence. This is an opportunity for the Headteacher to offer to take over these refreshments using catering staff and invite the committee to redeploy its largesse.

I see the Headteacher's role as being the person who encourages, welcomes, and thanks the PTA but equally helps the committee to realise that their contributions to school life are a bonus rather than a 'must have'. Serving the PTA should always be fun, something that each contributing parent should look forward to and thoroughly enjoy.

## Note

1   See Chapter 35 for further tips on what kind of benches to buy.

# 30 Finding balance and working with parents

For many Headteachers, dealing with complaining parents can be the most stressful and emotionally draining aspect of the job. Showing respect for schools, teachers, and Headteachers seems no longer to be part of UK society's value system. To get it back is going to require an enormous push, but the battle must start somewhere, and why not here – with you?

In the meantime, how do you retain some balance in the face of aggressive and personal attacks incoming from parents?

Interestingly, this problem is not new. In *The Republic*, Plato[1] advocates that parents should have very little to do with their children's education. Instead, the state dictates that children should be taught by those best suited to understand the principles of justice, virtue, and the good. He believed that philosophers were the ideal candidates for that job. Apart from the philosopher bit, the model he proposed has been in place since the Victorian period – the state essentially runs education, and parents act in support.

For whatever reason, that precept has been lost, and the problems caused by the new dynamic – a fundamental shift in parental attitudes – land squarely on the Headteacher.

The emotions the Headteacher is therefore dealing with revolve around the following:

- indignation at the belittling of status
- fury at irrational accusations of incompetence
- outrage at insinuations of a lack of professionalism
- incredulity at the hypocrisy of some parents who casually accuse the Headteacher of not caring
- feelings of oppression arising from demands for justice and retribution against other pupils
- despair at the lack of community spirit
- depression fuelled by the lack of any semblance of empathy for those worse off
- fear of complaints turning into physical violence
- dread of litigation based on the most tortuous and misguided interpretation of the Equality Act 2010
- loathing of patronising communications from those who would look down on the person and role of Headteacher

It's an exhaustive and exhausting list!

I confess that this is a bit of a rant, a dark journey through the worst of times, when achieving balance in the face of 'all that' seems impossible. We have to approach this aspect of finding balance with an acknowledgement that it really can get tough – very tough. From that acknowledgement, we can start to rebuild, to find strength and meaning from those tough moments. The key, initially at least, is not to let it grind you down – at least *not too much!* Of course you are going to be ground down a bit, and just admitting that is power in itself.

Once you have got through some of these tough times, it becomes possible to put them into a bank of self-affirmation. I literally cried at the beginning of my second Headship when I received a four-page letter from a parent telling me that she thought so little of me and the school that she felt her children weren't even safe. But . . . she had no actual cause to think that, and my response, heartfelt and passionate, put her mind at rest, and she became a firm advocate of the way I ran the school.

Each success, clutched from a burning furnace of molten, irrational nonsense, chiselled expertly, gently, and with huge finesse into a quiet acquiescence creates a jewel to look back on with pride.

**Don't let them grind you down; don't crumble. Dissipate their anger and rage with relentless kindness, boundless love, cast-iron rational thinking, and conflict resolution skills honed by every successful human interaction you've ever had.**

Every moment of conflict makes the Headteacher more complete, more competent, and more able to espouse the values they treasure and to execute their vision for the school and its pupils – and mostly for the pupils.

## Note

1  Plato, *The Republic*. Pub Penguin Classics, 2007.

# Part V: The Top Layer

# 31 Working with the Top Layer

The Top Layer is Governors, Trustees, Proprietors, Multi-Academy Trusts, and Local Authorities.

The types of people and/or organisations that sit strategically above the Headteacher and hold them to account are many and varied. The only Headteacher who does not have anyone above them is the sole proprietor acting as the Head of an independent school, and they are the exception to everything examined in this chapter.

Although it rarely feels like this, the buck doesn't actually stop at the Head's desk; it stops at the desk of the Top Layer. In overseeing the running of a school and the work of the Headteacher, all versions of the Top Layer have the following four concerns and mandates in common:

- To ensure the school is run according to the aims as stated in the Memorandums and Articles of Association ('Mem and Arts') or equivalent document.
- To ensure the school is compliant with the law and regulations.
- To ensure the school is run with financial prudence.
- To hire and, if necessary, fire the Headteacher.

## 'Mem and Arts' or equivalent document

All schools have some form of document which establishes the school as an entity, describes its governance structures, and lays out its purpose. This is where, for instance, a faith-based school will declare its religious allegiance, or a single-sex school will identify itself as such. The document will, in the case of an Academy operating within a Multi-Academy Trust, set out the 'Schemes of Delegation' detailing all the lines of accountability between the Local Governing Body of the school, the Board of Trustees of the Trust and the relationships between them and the Chief Executive Officer (CEO).

It is important that the Articles of Association are kept up to date and additional memorandums are drawn up when changes to the governing structure of the school arise. Scrutiny of the Articles by a new Headteacher can reveal anomalies which need to be ironed out. For instance, when I arrived at my second Headship, I found that there were many moments in the school week when acts of Christian worship were practised, exclusive of any other faiths. On reading the Articles, I found that the school was actually non-denominational – and so I dialled down on the Christianity.

## Compliance

Ensuring the school is compliant is a huge task and has become the role of full-time officers in school. According to one leading inspector of schools, the number of regulations has increased tenfold over the last 20 years. Given that ultimate responsibility for regulatory compliance lies with the Top Layer, this expansion of new laws has changed the way governance works in the UK. Governors and trustees are, on the whole, not paid. Before the role became seriously onerous, that worked fine, but now that they are expected to be knowledgeable and take responsibility for all these legal matters, it is harder to find people to take it on. So how does all this work in practice?

A few years ago, I was chatting with the Headteacher of a prestigious independent boarding school who commented that the Governing Body had smartened up its act a lot in recent years. I asked him how that had been achieved, and he said, "Upward delegation; I told them what to read, what to do, and when to do it."

Governance, then, is a funny old business! We have a group of unpaid volunteers who oversee the running of the school, holding to account the highest paid and most experienced member of the organisation. At the same time, that most senior person has to guide and inform the Governors *how* to do that. You would imagine that the opportunities for corrupt practice were rife – and yet, in a curious and illogical way, it does work. It works because those volunteers are naturally diligent, inquisitive, and want to make a difference; if they didn't, they wouldn't be there.

Another seeming anomaly is that Governing Bodies and Boards of Trustees are populated mostly by non-educators. People from all walks of life bring their expertise and world views to the table. If the mix of skills is right, then you end up with a powerful forum, able to debate each challenge the school faces from multiple angles. The quest to find a suitable cross-section of professional skills to add to the Board is largely, I think, a red herring. It can be useful to have a lawyer, accountant, architect, builder, academic, etc., on the Board, but those people are not there necessarily to contribute from their professional backgrounds. They are there to govern – with the four imperatives discussed earlier at the forefront of their thinking. Neither is it the role, say, of an accountant Governor to get directly involved in auditing or accounting – the school pays people to do that – the accountant Governor's role is to ensure that they do the job well.

The best Governors are people with vision, courage, compassion, and empathy. Without doubt, the best Governor I ever had the privilege to work with was a poet. She was insightful, unafraid to turn a debate on its head with a single remark, and she always championed the pupils.

### Hire and fire the Head

The Headteacher has a boss – and that boss is the Top Layer. Whereas the relationship each Headteacher has with their employees is clearly defined, the relationship between the Top Layer and the Headteacher is much more negotiable.

There is a wide variety of ways this relationship plays out. In schools where there is a Top Layer which is responsible only for that one school, it's all about trust. The Headteacher will guide the Governors to ensure that they can perform their role in relation to compliance effectively and, in turn, the Governors will build their trust in the Head's competence. For their part, the Headteacher will build trust that the Governors are committed to the vision and values as presented at interview and subsequent reviews and updates. The two parties move forward in mutual support with the benefit of the school and its pupils as their driving force.

At a school that is part of a group of schools or MAT, the Top Layer may well be more directive, so Headship at these schools feels more like being an employee than the top-ranked leader. The question then becomes: *who is running the school?* If the Top Layer effectively runs the school, then that puts the Headteacher (and the Local Governing Body, if there is one) in an anomalous position in relation to governmental accountability as delivered by inspection. Until very recently, Top Layers of groups of schools and MATs were not inspected per se – it was only the schools within the groups that were inspected. That meant that Headteachers were being made accountable to inspectors for policies and funding decisions that they themselves did not make and may indeed have disagreed with; the people who made those decisions were unaccountable.

## Operational vs strategic

There can be moments when the Top Layer, for the best of motives, starts to interfere. For instance, a retired teacher on the Board gets involved in curriculum design and starts to hold meetings with teachers about pedagogy and resources. This can be very awkward for the Headteacher because the Governor in question is, in effect, their employer. The Headteacher is conflicted in attempting to influence the Governor to step away from influencing teachers in the school. The way to separate the roles of Headteacher and Governors is to ask whether the point of debate is 'operational' or 'strategic'. So, in the case of the interfering retired teacher, the Headteacher can intervene with the following:

> I am very interested in your ideas for developing pedagogy but this is strictly an operational matter – not strategic. I suggest the way forward is for the two of us to meet so you can share your ideas with me, and I can take things forward from there.

## Conclusion

The best way to run a school is for the Headteacher to have accountable autonomy. The autonomy is limited by a Top Layer who scrutinise, guide, and advise and who are ultimately empowered to step in to fire the Head if necessary. In many MATs and groups of schools, this model has been replaced by the professional governance: any putative Headteacher should consider carefully which model they wish to work under before applying for their next post.

# 32 Integrating the Top Layer with the school

As we saw in the last chapter, the shape and structure of the Top Layers overseeing schools is a complex picture, but in one way or another, there is usually a body of people directly connected to each individual school. Where that is the case – let's call it local governance – there is an expectation that the Governors will be formally integrated into the school. Regulations dictate that there must be a Governor assigned specifically to oversee safeguarding. Care needs to be taken nonetheless, because safeguarding will always be the responsibility of every adult involved in the school, and it is a mistake to think that having a Safeguarding Governor in any way excuses anyone else from taking it equally seriously. Whilst the Safeguarding Governor is there to scrutinise and support the work of the safeguarding team within the school, it is the duty of the other Governors to scrutinise and support the work of the Safeguarding Governor.

For local governance to be most effective, Governors need to know the staff and the staff need to know the Governors. Finding ways to achieve this is never easy, and the bigger the school, the harder it is. Here are some ideas.

## Governor Days

Once – maybe even twice – a year, a day is agreed for the Governors to visit the school formally. (It is important to acknowledge here that Governors have the absolute right to visit the school at any time they choose and don't need an invitation to do so. It is courteous if the Governors contact the school before visiting, but they don't have to. This is all to ensure that the Headteacher is held properly to account and can't manipulate the visits Governors make.)

The Headteacher might put together a programme for a Governor Day of lesson drop-ins and meetings – or the Governors may just be allowed to roam free through the school. In my experience, a mixture of both was most useful. It is good practice to set aside a suitable amount of time towards the end of the day for Governors to collate their findings, based on their experience of the day, and then report back to the Head and SLT. The discussion should be minuted and filed with formal governance papers to demonstrate to inspectors the level of scrutiny that has been achieved.

Governor Days might also include opportunities for staff to meet and get to know the Governors. An informal gathering can be a very useful way to further integrate the Board.

When dropping into lessons, it is important Governors fully understand their role. Whether or not the Governor is an educationalist, they're not there to *judge*. The role is subtle: no notes should be taken in the lesson, and no judgements about the quality of teaching and learning should be made. If the observing Governor has doubts or concerns, they should discuss these fully with the Headteacher, who can then provide context and follow up if necessary. The objective of the lesson observation is to help fulfil the Governors' core purpose – to ensure the school is being run in accordance with the Articles of Association and that the school is compliant with regulation – and nothing else. Anything beyond that is operational: much offence and trouble can be caused by a Governor who strays outside this brief.

To create some more focus to the lesson drop-ins, the Headteacher may opt to tie the event into relevant aspects of the SDP. For example, the plan may include an emphasis on open questioning and the development of oracy skills, and Governors may be asked to look out for examples. That doesn't mean, however, that those elements may necessarily be included in the lessons they attend.

## Checking for compliance

Governor visits can be useful in providing evidence for compliance, particularly in the area of pastoral care and safeguarding. The Headteacher might provide Governors with questions to ask pupils and staff. For example, for staff: "Do you know who all the DSL and DDSLs are and how to get in touch with them?" or "In what circumstances would you go directly to the police to report an incident?" For pupils: "Who would you talk to if you had a problem at home and needed the support of a different adult?"

Useful work can be done before a Governor visit to check the long list of compliance aspects that Governors should be aware of so that the right questions can be asked. Ultimately, these visits are about triangulating the reports from the Headteacher. When inspectors ask the Governors how they know the school is compliant, it is not sufficient for them to say, "Because the Headteacher tells us it is." They need to know for themselves.

If Governor Days prove too hard to arrange, there is no harm in having visits from individuals. The individual Governor might then report back to the board at the next general meeting.

## Sub-committees

Most Governing Bodies divide themselves into sub-committees in order to spread the workload. The sub-committees report into the main body through verbal and written reviews. The remit of sub-committees can vary but usually include Finance (including salary awards), Grounds and Buildings, Academic, Personnel, and Safeguarding. The Governors might want to invite senior leaders and staff to sub-committee meetings – the obvious example being the invitation for the Finance Officer to attend the Finance Committee. (It is important, however, that the Governors do not act as the line manager of the Finance Officer: that role is the preserve of the Headteacher. Governing Bodies that manage the Finance Officer directly can cause mistrust to form between them and the Head.)

A good integration idea is to invite individual members of staff to make presentations to the Governor about specific projects they are working on, or simply to update the Board on their subject area. Governors usually find this exercise exciting because it brings them closer to the core activities of the daily life of the school.

## Workload

There is a lot for each Governor to get through: simply reading all the prepared papers can be an onerous task in itself. Colour coding papers into 'must read', 'important', and 'good to know' can help Governors distribute their time effectively. It seems rather obvious, but getting the technology right is also an important way to support the work Governors have to do. Providing papers in a simple 'one-click' format will mean that they can download information quickly and easily. Once inside the files, the papers need to be clearly headed and indexed.

## Guiding the meetings

We have seen the importance of the Headteacher being confident to delegate upwards and provide clear guidance for how meetings need to be conducted. Most Chairs will seek guidance, so having a professional Clerk to the Governors is very useful. A professional Clerk will take and distribute the minutes but will also be able to answer technical questions – like whether an idea needs a motion and vote or how long a Governor can serve before re-election. The Headteacher should sit on all sub-committees, and meetings should not be held if, for some reason, the Head cannot attend.

The relationship between the Headteacher and Chair of Governors is pivotal, even if there is another 'layer' of governance above the Chair. The Chair should act as the 'critical friend' – there to support and help but also guide and question. No Chair or Head can guarantee they are going to get on well, but the relationship should never fall short of courteous and professional. How the Headteacher goes about forming a trusting relationship with the Chair and individual Governors is part of their vision for how the school is run.

Some Chairs like to set time limits on discussions; others like them to be loose and informal. There is a tricky balance to be struck between keeping focus whilst also allowing the discussion to go where it needs to go. Perhaps a good rule of thumb is that meetings that go beyond two hours are probably not very effective.

The minutes of meetings should be checked for accuracy by the Headteacher first, before being scrutinised and signed off by the Governors.

## Summary

There are lots of ways to integrate the Governing Body with the school, and the most important focus should be on ensuring it happens and is effective. In practice, one of the key functions of this version of the Top Layer is to steady the ship in times of trouble and turbulence. Things can 'happen' – the Headteacher falls ill and cannot continue, there is a scandal involving a teacher, government funding arrangements alter, and fundamental changes are needed to the Articles of Association. All these are examples of where the Governing Body comes into its own, and it is in such moments that the community – parents, teachers, and pupils – need to be able to trust that the Governors are knowledgeable and have the competencies and capacity to cope.

# 33 Finding balance and working with the Top Layer

Although working with the Top Layer is usually less time consuming than working with the other three estates, the stress that arises from a conflictual relationship can be extreme – for the simple reason that they are the Headteacher's employer and have the power to dismiss. Working with the Top Layer is often an area of Headship which is hardest to gain experience of before taking up the role.

Establishing trusting relationships with the Top Layer is a little like paying insurance premiums. The Top Layer is often the structural mechanism which stabilises the school in the event of shock. Therefore, the balance the Headteacher can cultivate here is to ensure their vision and the vision of the Top Layer are in step.

The chapters on balance at the end of each Part of this book have looked at establishing wellbeing in relation to pupils, staff, and parents. But what if they all go wrong at the same time? What if a death in the family coincides with alarming personal biopsy results, a pupil dies, a parent physically attacks a member of staff, other staff go on strike, and news leaks out that someone from the Top Layer has embezzled school funds – what if all these happen in the same week?!

Cue the trusted Governors/Trustees/Proprietor/MAT/Local Authority. Stepping in at times like this is their role, and the Headteacher has every right to lean on these people heavily in such circumstances. These are also circumstances in which having membership of a Headteachers union would be vital.

## A guardian role for the Top Layer

The Top Layer, or perhaps someone specifically from that entity, should be assigned to look after the Headteacher. The Head is at risk of burnout as much as any other employee of the school – perhaps more so. No matter how emotionally and psychologically robust the Headteacher is, if the job is overwhelming then they won't survive. Whilst it is the Head themselves who can and should define a version of leadership that is sustainable, it is also the job of the Top Layer to monitor that, listen, and act if things start to tip the wrong way. Equally, the Headteacher has the responsibility to themselves *and* the school to allow the Top Layer to intervene if they are not coping. The Headteacher needs to heed the words of in-flight cabin crew: "Apply the oxygen mask to yourself first before trying to help others."

DOI: 10.4324/9781003517825-38

## Summary

This is the fifth and final chapter in this book to examine finding balance and wellbeing. It might therefore be useful to try to summarise all these thoughts into a simple maxim – a mantra, if you like – that Headteachers can carry with them:

> For all the altruistic, noble, and child-centred precepts the Headteacher embodies, they are of no use to anyone if they don't look after themselves first. There will be times when the **professional** thing to do is to be at home, distracting themselves with something they enjoy, relaxing, and restoring.

# 34 Fifth estate – inspectors

## Accountability

I have deliberately described how school is divided into *four* estates and then added a *fifth* rather perversely! The idea of inspector accountability can feel like that. The inspectorate is unmanageable; the school has no say over the criteria, timing, level, or area of scrutiny. Having been both inspector and inspected, I can share that inspection rarely feels fair or proportionate. It is largely something the school has to get through, doing its best.

## Disassociate

If there was ever a time to disassociate from the school, this is it. Headship is a job; the Headteacher is the leader *for now* and will at some point hand the baton over to the next incumbent. The next Head might well tear up everything the current Head has put in place and change the school out of all recognition. The anticipation of inspection is usually the worst bit, so the Headteacher should use their CBT techniques consistently to reduce anxiety and stress.

## Some tips on how to prepare for inspection

- Start by knowing as much as possible. As reading and research is undertaken, the Headteacher must divide preparation work into manageable chunks. Just getting on top of compliance is a huge task, so the Headteacher needs to delegate some of this work to other competent employees while ensure they are reasonably knowledgeable themselves. The review of policies in relation to compliance will take many focused sessions, so working from home is thoroughly justified.
- Distribute tasks to members of the leadership team, but make sure they actually have the capacity to take on this work.
- The Headteacher needs to model the calmness they expect to see in their staff.
- During the inspection, the Headteacher needs to challenge the Lead Inspector whenever necessary. All inspection frameworks are incredibly condensed, designed only to provide a snapshot of school life. It is therefore easy for inspectors to get the wrong impression, and the Headteacher needs to step in, create space for additional evidence to be gathered and presented, and argue every point. **The Headteacher will not gain credit for the school by being easy to work with.** Whilst being respectful and professional, the Head should enter the period of inspection prepared to strain every sinew to ensure that the evidence inspectors see is an accurate reflection of the best the school has to offer. Raising reasonable challenges to every negative judgement will ensure that inspectors are doubly certain that their opinion is based on the balance of verifiable evidence.
- Brief staff and pupils about the best way to support the inspectors and the school. It would be nice to think that an inspection visit unfolds whilst everyday life for teachers

and pupils carries on as normal. That is not how it works! The race to find evidence to substantiate judgements is not just between the inspectors and the clock – it's a race between the inspectors and the school as well. The Headteacher should be telling staff and pupils how to answer questions to elicit the best reaction from the inspectors. That's not being cynical at all – it is good advice, because inspectors need to find verbatim evidence to support a judgement. A staff member who feels it's indelicate to boast may end up underplaying some great achievements and damage the inspection result. Pupils will do as they please no matter what the Headteacher asks them to say, but if they have been briefed, then at least the school has a better chance of some un-ironic straight talking from the teenagers.

- Inspection has a framework and is formally ruled by protocol and rules; it's pragmatic and expedient. The time frame is unmovable, and from the inspectors' point of view, the job has to be done on time with few excuses or riders allowed. That gives the school the opportunity to sow seeds of doubt about negative judgements, working the game in their favour whenever they can. Again, this may sound cynical, but inspection is a high-stakes event where jobs, livelihoods, and the ongoing pride in the quality of pupils' education are at stake. There is no room for scruples; ruthlessness – on behalf of the children – is entirely justified.

# Part VI: Conclusion

# 35 The really useful chapter

You may find that the tips contained in this chapter are the best or the worst part of the book. There are a lot of things that a new Headteacher might well not know about before they start the job. The following are things I wish I had known before I made the mistakes that I did. On the other hand, you may know all of it – in which case, well done!

In no particular order:

- Don't ask employees in their early to mid-20s to do things they aren't ready for. They are adults but not necessarily ready for a lot of responsibility. I think you should always regard them as people for whom you might need to make reasonable adjustments.
- Start all evening events at one set time, e.g. 7:00pm. The community soon learn that there is no need to ring the school to find out when the meeting/concert/performance, etc., is. It's *always* at the same time.
- Don't stint on the biscuits or make staff pay for their coffee. The budget is never that tight that showing staff you appreciate them is worth the saving. It doesn't happen in other sectors, and it shouldn't happen in education. The same goes for washing up at lunch break or the end of the day. Put it on the job list for the caretakers – let the teachers and assistants off the hook.
- Attend the Christmas Party, but leave once the meal and any formalities are over. There's nothing more cringing than watching your employees gradually getting the worse for a few drinks. That may be just my take on this, but hey.
- Be as transparent as you can about the financial state of the school. All your employees have a stake in understanding how money is being allocated, and it will prevent rumours and resentment. If the school is struggling due to underfunding, remain positive and be open about the solutions you are pursuing. If you want to delegate this communication (better as a speech, to be honest) to the Bursar/Finance Officer, that is fine, but be sure you can trust them not to scaremonger or come across as defensive.
- Although the Bursar/Finance Officer is the administrator of the money, they are not *in charge* of the money. They work for you, not in parallel; they can't overrule you, but you can overrule them. They may have a direct line to the Top Layer, but they still work for you.
- Your school should smell good. If the toilets smell, sort them out with automatic aroma sprays. If the area around the canteen smells of cabbage at lunchtime, fit better ventilation. No horrible smells, no excuses.
- There should always be someone with full DSL training on site when children are present. It is usually a good idea (not always) for the Headteacher to sit strategically above the DSL and DDSLs. The Headteacher is fully trained too but can then act as a line manager.
- When you are interviewing anyone who is going to be in 'regulated activity', you must take notes. The notes should be cogent and legible, and they must include a safeguarding question and the answer given. You need also to record your *judgement* of whether

you considered the answer to the safeguarding question to be adequate or not. The notes should be signed and dated and kept with the applicant's file if successful.
- Some Headteachers like to keep all the papers relating to applicants and interviewees. It is sensible to keep the interview notes of unsuccessful interviews for a month or so in case they wish to challenge the decision under the Equality Act 2010. Then, to be compliant with GDPR, you should destroy all these papers and record that you have done so. Applications from people you choose not to interview should be destroyed unless you have a justification to keep them 'on file'.
- If you write things about someone and in retrospect feel you would rather that person didn't see what you've written, you *can* delete those written records or emails unless they have made an SAR.
- If you receive a challenging email, a complaint, or just a communication which is aggressive and demanding, don't forget that a 'holding email' is a perfectly legitimate and appropriate response. Just because the person on the other end is demanding a response that day doesn't mean you have to give that response. This is excellent advice to give to staff as well, and you should also tell staff that they can say '*someone*' will get back to the correspondent within xx hours (48 hours is not unreasonable).
- Don't always be the first to arrive and the last to leave. It sends a signal that you probably haven't got your own work/life balance sorted yet. Whilst you may be able to cope with the hours you're working, setting this example may lead others to follow suit – and they may end up burning out.
- Sometimes, the best way to lead is by doing nothing. Beware jumping in because you feel the need to be seen and heard responding to an issue. Delaying your response – or, indeed, just not responding – can be a powerful mechanism to take the sting out of a difficult situation.
- The school's insurance broker will visit the school annually to ensure that the leadership is happy with the cover and update them on changes. It is well worth attending those meetings, even if that means badgering the Top Layer to let you be there. It is important to know what the school is insured against and how the policies work in practice. When I experienced the disaster described in Chapter 22, I had just met with the insurance broker and was therefore aware that the school was entitled to claim £10,000 worth of PR work. That proved invaluable because without that knowledge, it probably would not have occurred to me to engage a PR company.
- Does the school spend more on cleaning than it does on teaching resources? If so, is that something the Headteacher is content with?
- Always know what you want to get out of a meeting before you go in.
- Whether or not the Headteacher teaches is dependent on several factors, including a gap in the staffing analysis and subject knowledge. The Headteacher who carries on teaching does carry some kudos in the staff room and retains an ongoing experience of life in the classroom. It is also a good way to get to know the new intake of pupils each year – so, Reception in a primary school and Year 7 in a secondary school.
- Primary school classroom teachers are entitled to around two and a half hours of Planning Preparation and Assessment time (PPA) per week. In many schools, PPA is taken in one block and the school employs someone to cover that time. Instead, consider

employing specialist sports and music teachers so that the classroom teacher takes their PPA time when those lessons are being taught.
- If you are buying benches for the playground, bear in mind that children, especially adolescents, don't tend to 'sit' on a bench – they climb all over them, often testing them to destruction. So, the sort of benches you might find in a public park, with back rests and arms, are not suitable. Instead, a thick plank on two sturdy legs, concreted into the ground, is best.
- Wherever your school is located, it's a part of a local community. Creating links and working closely with that community is something some schools do well and others ignore. There are huge and far-reaching benefits to making as many close links with the community as possible, whether that is the Local Authority, Chamber of Commerce, other schools – both state and independent – or any aspect of local life which connects the school to the families of the pupils who attend. Every connection is a possible source of support, additional funding, good will, and help.

# 36 Is it all worth it? – A personal summary

There is no doubt that running a school is tough. It can challenge you on physical, emotional, intellectual, and social levels. But if you have the aptitude, ambition and courage, then it is the best job in education.

I enjoyed Headship. Working with people is fun and I shared many life-enhancing moments of humour and joy with staff, parents, and pupils. The Head is uniquely placed to make a real difference to the lives of people in all four estates. Everyone in the school community knows you and, if you get the job right, will appreciate the contribution you make to their lives. That is unique and special. I didn't expect lots of plaudits, and I tried to be a servant leader. I was interested only in succeeding by facilitating the success of others.

I enjoyed the creative opportunities that Headship brings. Reading other educators' ideas, adding my own, and turning these ideas into reality was a thrill like no other. I built two new buildings and refurbished many others, and I relished the challenges each time. I was able to lead on teaching and learning and provide novel frameworks for both pupils and teachers to explore. I saw results, behaviour and engagement improve; I delighted in seeing diffidence and cynicism subside.

It was exciting and gratifying to be able to facilitate outreach programmes that benefitted the pupils of dozens of local schools. This enabled me to evolve the values and vision of the school to include a keen sense of moral purpose. The school was there not just to serve the pupils and their families but to also make a meaningful contribution to the wider community across the city.

I was also fortunate that my Top Layer had enough faith in me to allow me to develop my educational thinking to where it has made a difference both nationally and across the world. *Girls on Board* – which is my project to empower girls to manage the dynamics of their friendships for themselves – was initially funded by (and later re-paid to) the school. The *Girls on Board* approach has now been adopted by more than 1,000 schools across the globe. Hundreds of thousands of girls have benefitted and the project is very much ongoing. I could not have generated the ideas for *Girls on Board* unless I had been a Headteacher, and the 18 years I served have given me the crucial credibility to evangelise and promote the approach.

*Girls on Board* led me to write *Working with Boys* about the challenge of guiding boys in school to be the best they can be. Helping both educators and parents to understand the drivers that lead some boys to be under-motivated and to underachieve has been rewarding. The ultimate goal is to see the ideas in the book adopted in a society-wide crusade to end harmful sexual behaviour in schools.

Headship is the pinnacle of the profession, but extraordinary opportunities can follow. I look back on my time with pride and, inevitably, the odd tinge of regret. Should I have stepped away when I did? If I had been more confident in my own abilities in my early years, could I have achieved more, sooner?

Ultimately, my career in school leadership has equipped me to write this book: *How to Run a School*. My passion for education is undiminished, and if this book contributes to better educational outcomes for pupils even in small ways, then it has been worth it.

# Postscript

# 37 How to run an education system

As the arguments swirl and mutate around equal access to good education for the next generation, one glaring fact goes unnoticed – you get the system you are prepared to pay for. There should be no need for arguments about school types or equality of opportunity because every school – and that includes the one nearest to you – should be a great school.

The education system in the UK is run by politicians and is therefore prone to variations in ideological approaches which rarely, if ever, meet the needs of the sector. Education has a Top Layer of its own – in the shape of the Department for Education (DfE) which is led by the Secretary of State for Education, a Cabinet position. There are various problems with the way this Top Layer operates, and those problems affect every single educational establishment in the country.

## Secretary of State is not an educator

Anyone looking in from the outside would probably be astonished to realise that the person with the most power and influence over education is not, and never has been, an educator. There is no requirement for the Secretary of State to have had experience in the classroom or been involved at Local Authority level in supporting schools – or any qualification of any sort. They are lay, untrained politicians who have been assigned the Education brief without necessarily even asking for it.

If challenged, they'd probably argue that they spent 13 years in schools themselves and that those experiences (30 or 40 years earlier) qualify them handsomely to do the job. I've been to the supermarket thousands of times, but I wouldn't pretend to know how to run one!

## Stepping stone to more senior roles

The Prime Minister of the day will often appoint as Secretary of State for Education a member of the reigning political party who is regarded as 'up and coming' – a talent to be nurtured for future more senior roles in government. The incumbent will, for their part, realise that they probably have around 1-2 years[1] to make a difference before being moved on. If they have been seen to have succeeded by their political masters, then the next move will be a promotion; if not, then they may well drop out of government altogether and return to the back benches. With so little time to gain a working knowledge of education and yet needing to change things to make a difference, the Secretary of State often opts for simple answers to complex questions. They are usually most influenced by other party members in government and on the back benches and pay little or no attention to the voice of educators.

As an example of Top Layer governance, the current Secretary of State model performs badly, leading to policy changes which are ill considered and motivated by political self-interest. Over time, the course steered by these ever-changing 'captains' of education is a wiggling line with no sense of strategic direction. The Top Layer is operational in the worst possible sense, and the inherent structure of this governance model mitigates against any meaningful long-term strategic view. Since the end of WWII, only three Secretaries of State have served more than four years in post.[2] None has achieved five years.

### How can we fix this?

The appointment of the Secretary of State should be reserved, by law, for someone with educational qualifications and teaching experience. The role should also come with an expectation that it will last for the full five-year term of a Parliament. This would then encourage teachers and senior school leaders to enter politics, knowing that they had at least a chance of being promoted to Secretary of State. That would attract educators with a real and authentic passion to improve the system. This feels eminently feasible; the only thing standing in the way is tradition and a lack of imagination and political will.

## Who are the civil servants and advisers?

Having been around the senior echelons of schools for more than 20 years, I have only ever met one person who worked at the DfE – and that was over dinner at a conference. Yet the DfE employs around 4,000 people.[3] There is vast, accumulated wisdom amongst the civil servants who advise the Secretary of State, but very few people in schools know who they are and whether they ever taught in or led a school. There is a serious lack of transparency about their backgrounds and suitability.

### How can we fix this?

The DfE should undertake a major drive for transparency so that educators can understand and relate to the people who run the system. In turn, the staff at the DfE should be visiting more schools, talking at conferences, and making themselves open to discussion and debate.

## The curriculum is out of date

Pupils in the schools I ran would often question the relevance of the curriculum. They complained how removed it felt from the skills and knowledge they believed that they needed to succeed in life. How we might go about a wholesale revision of the curriculum is the subject of an entire book in itself. There are too many questions to answer to do this topic justice, but here are just a few. They're all controversial!

- Do we really need so much maths on the timetable? Is the maths curriculum content beyond Year 6 useful and relevant?
- In a global society that speaks a lot of English, and with cheap, instant digital translators, is the amount of time dedicated to teaching MFL to young people justified?
- Why is there a hierarchy of subjects? Is science really more important than art, music, or drama?
- Why is PSHE given so little priority on the timetable? Aren't its contents amongst the most important that schools teach? PSHE includes philosophy, politics, and relationships and sex education, along with a whole raft of important life skills lessons, and yet it is squashed into one lesson a week or, worse still, a single 'drop down' day a year. In

my experience, when PSHE is taught well, it is the subject pupils most look forward to because it is relevant, immediate, and useful.

## The curriculum is driven by the exam system

Before we ask how we can fix the curriculum, we need to acknowledge that nothing will change until the thing that drives it changes – and that is the **examination system**. From Reception onwards, pupils are taught to pass standardised testing at KS2 SATs, and public exams at the GCSE and A levels (and vocational qualifications post 16). Not only is the examination system the tail that wags the dog, but embedded within that system is a pernicious obsession with **rank order**. At no point in adult life are people subjected to such a brutal ranking system, and they wouldn't put up with it if they were.

The rank ordering of pupils is justified by the selection needs of universities and colleges. Employers, too, are interested in the grades achieved, though often they prefer to make appointments based on interviewing and aptitude tests. It seems to me that the selection needs of employers, universities, and colleges are the fleas that bite the tail that wags the dog.

Pupils are placed in rank order by the exam grades they achieve. As an illustration of how inappropriate our current grading system is, let's look at the grade ranges of public examinations.

At KS2 SATs, the range of marks awarded goes from 80-120, averaged out across three topic areas, so that is a 41-point granulation.

At GCSE, grading ranges from 9-1, plus U. There are various ways in which the grades across multiple subjects are averaged out, and they are often arcane and disadvantageous to pupils who choose subjects that are not considered serious or mainstream. So, that is a 10-point granulation with lots of complications added in.

At A level, grading ranges from A* to U – an 8-point granulation across usually three subject areas. These grades, along with the vocational qualifications, are converted into Universities and Colleges Admissions Services (UCAS) points. Some, but not all, universities admit on the basis of UCAS points, which can be added to by passing, for example, music grades on an instrument or voice.

Interestingly, the further up the academic ladder you go, the narrower the grading range becomes. At degree level, there is a 5-point range from 1st to 2:1 to 2:22 to 3rd plus 'Ordinary'. At the master's level and beyond, it finally becomes pass or fail.

The exam system is high stakes, arcane, and exceptionally rigid and is used in a way which is divisive and promotes inequality. Society has come to accept it as immutable. For many pupils, exams are a *sliding doors* moment – just one more mark in that GCSE Art exam and the overall point score would have been enough to gain entrance to the academically elite 6th-form college, but with the scores as they are, community college is the remaining option.

### *How can we fix this?*

To fix the curriculum, we need to release teachers and pupils from the chains of rigid examination based on the rank ordering of our young population. We should design a curriculum that produces well-educated and emotionally intelligent citizens capable of making contributions to society based on values that work for everyone, with no one left behind.

What follows is radical, but only because what I am suggesting is such a long way from where we are now. What if the end of school was marked by matriculation accompanied by a rich and meaningful record of achievement? There would be a pass or fail aspect to matriculation, but the only reason a pupil would fail would be if they wilfully refused to be educated.

The two strongest arguments against this are the following:

- Adults who are not educators will be very hard to convince, especially the more influential members of society – in other words, the ones who did well in school and benefitted from being judged against the criteria which placed them at the top of the rank ordering system. This is not an argument against a matriculation per se, more that changing the system would be an almighty battle against a hierarchy which education has created and supported for centuries.
- People will argue that aspiring to the best grades in public exams is motivational and that if you take that away, pupils will drift through school aimlessly. There's a plethora of unproven theories behind the idea that people only do their best in order to be rewarded and that grades represent the ultimate reward. This is the argument between extrinsic and intrinsic rewards systems which I looked at in detail in Chapter 4. Motivation is complex and nuanced, and to build an entire education system on the assumption that pupils will only work hard for extrinsic reward just doesn't hold up in the face of the evidence, as Dan Pink proved in his book *Drive*.[4] In any case, matriculation would contain some testing; it's just that it would become part of a broader portfolio rather than the sole indicator of achievement.

The bottom line is that the current system automatically and by definition brands a proportion of pupils as failures. They have failed because their marks in public exams, especially GCSE, fall below a watermark that has been assigned – by norm referencing[5] – to the bottom 10-20% of the pupil population graduating Year 11. They may have failed because they did not apply themselves diligently enough to their studies, but they are much more likely to have failed because they were not born with a brain suited to the curriculum and its testing system. Einstein himself did not do well at school!

As I say, this is a radical argument, but its implementation is only limited by our lack of imagination to see the universal benefits that would be reaped from such a change. Let employers and higher education make up their own selection tests – educators can then get on with teaching pupils to be the best they can be.

## Get rid of ideological drivers

One of the main ideological drivers behind the examination system is neo-liberalism. This philosophy of economics focuses on the reduction of the size of the state and the marketisation of commerce, coupled with de-regulation. This then allows competition to drive the best economic results for a country. Neo-liberalism has mutated and has been applied to various parts of life for which it was never intended – education being one of them. Judging schools through inspection has created the idea of 'good' schools and 'bad' schools. The partial marketisation of admissions into schools then means that 'bad' schools will lose pupils to the 'good' schools. The idea is that, in responding to this competition, the 'bad' schools strive to do better so they can attract more pupils and therefore more funding.

The introduction of market economy thinking into the education sector has been a disaster for two reasons:

1. For the forces of competition to work, there must be spare capacity in the system, and quite a lot of it. If parents are going to transfer their children from the 'bad' school to the 'good' school, then the 'good' school must have spare places to accommodate them. But spare capacity is inefficient and costly. For a while, the 'bad' school will have empty classrooms and contracted teachers that need to be made redundant. This is an unaffordable and bad way to run a school system, and it doesn't work. Without spare capacity in the 'good' schools, pupils are forced to remain in the 'bad' school - which becomes worse and worse because it quickly gains a reputation for being the school no one wants to attend. So the basic mechanism which facilitates improvement through competition ceases to exist.
The state sector has never had the kind of spare capacity that would make this system work. Local Authorities (who oversee admissions) are told by the DfE to run schools in their area at 98%+ full.
2. Comparing schools, even ones quite close to each other, is a silly idea. Comparing an all-boys non-selective Catholic school to a highly selective all-girls grammar school, even though they are neighbours, is like comparing Thursday with a piece of string. But imagine working at or attending a school which you are told - whether by a single-word judgement or by some other equally derogatory and condemnatory method - is a 'bad' school. How does that motivate the teacher who has dedicated their working life to that school and was, until that moment, proud of their career? How does that help the pupils of that school whose identity is wrapped up in the uniform and logo which they had previously wore with such excitement? It doesn't - it's a horrendous system!

### How can we fix this?

Treat each school as a noble and self-improving entity which needs support, guidance, and proper funding. Whilst parents will always talk about comparisons between the schools available to their children, there is no need for the state to amplify and solidify those comparisons - it's not helpful.

### Inspection makes things worse

At the heart of the neo-liberal ideas that have proved so corrosive to the education system has been inspection. Judging a school is not only subject to politically driven interpretations of what we might mean by 'good', but it is also a deeply unhelpful activity.

### How can we fix this?

Inspection needs to be supportive, compassionate, and focused on producing the best outcomes for pupils **now**. The way inspection currently seeks to improve schools is by judging and condemning schools first and then requiring senior leaders to meet targets in order to receive a better judgement. In the meantime, the Headteacher often loses their job or resigns, leaving the school even worse off than the day before the inspectors called. The inspection framework needs to be based on the idea that the morning after their visit will be a better day for the school than the day before they arrived. That is achieved by supportive, constructive guidance leading to immediate, medium-term, and long-term improvements.

## Funding

If we want an education system we are proud of, then government should ring fence a percentage of gross domestic product (GDP) to be spent on education and commit to a capital expenditure budget that would see all school buildings replaced in the next 20 years.

If we want the best people to be teachers, then the government needs to show some respect by paying them a wage that reflects their significance to the nation.

If we want the best educational experience for pupils, then class sizes need to be closer to 25 than 30.

Money spent by government on education should not be seen as a cost but as an investment.

## Invest in leadership

Leadership is everything and always has been. Good leaders run good schools, so reverse the funding cuts to leadership training and re-establish the National College of School Leadership.

## Rein in parental influence

The government should put some sensible restrictions on parental influence by formally empowering Headteachers to demand the highest standards of behaviour from them.

## Standards in public life

Our experience of dishonesty and corruption in central government during and since the Brexit Referendum has led to an erosion of respect for authority and the rule of law in general. This has had a knock-on effect on pupil behaviour and has fuelled the lack of respect parents show to schools and teachers. We need to improve the standards of behaviour in public life, hold our politicians to account for their corrupt actions, and restore some sense of dignity in the way we regard our political leaders.

## What schools should not have to do

The cuts in budgets to children's services, particularly social workers and mental health professionals, has placed huge pressure on schools. There are many circumstances which in the past would have been dealt with by an agency external to schools but which are now expected to be dealt with by teachers and pastoral support workers. Not only that, but those services are also overwhelmed and unable to treat young people before they become seriously ill, or support families before disaster strikes. As Andy Phippen[6] points out:

> We're becoming stuck in a vicious circle of professionals with increasingly complex cases having less time to give to less complex young people. These young people therefore don't

get appropriate and timely support, meaning they engage in more risky behaviours, leading them to become more complex if and when they eventually become eligible for support.

### *How can we fix this?*

Funding for services for young people needs to return to the level at which early intervention can be achieved. This model still exists in medicine. For instance, the way GPs are funded leans heavily on preventative consultation: "Come and see us with a small thing before it becomes a big thing" is echoed in all surgeries. The National Health Service, for all its unfolding issues, still makes the argument to politicians that this approach is justified both ethically and economically – it costs more to treat the seriously ill. But the same argument has not been successfully made when it comes to a range of services that are used to support children in school. The 'cost' is then witnessed in the additional suffering it causes children because they are being treated and supported by people in school with sub-optimal training. School budgets, which are already stretched, now have to afford mental health workers and large pastoral teams acting as counsellors and social workers.

UK society has a confused attitude towards spending money on children. For instance, many people feel it is simply unfair to even be *allowed* to spend money on your children's education. There is a desire to level down based on envy. On the other hand, some people argue that selective state-funded schools are a great way to promote social mobility, even though those schools are mostly populated by families who can afford to live in the catchment area and who pay for tuition to pass the admissions exam.

Like many state-run services, it comes down to money. Few doubt that education is underfunded, but finding the money is always hard when there are many competing needs. Money, however, is generated by creating by a population that is well educated, keen to work hard for themselves and the greater good, able to innovate and collaborate, and happy to play their part.

We can do better than this.

## Notes

1. The average length of service of a Secretary of State for Education in the last 50 years is around 20 months.
2. Keith Joseph, David Blunkett, and Michael Gove.
3. www.gov.uk/government/publications/department-for-education-staff-numbers/department-for-education-staff-numbers
4. Dan Pink, *Drive*. Pub Canongate Books, 2018.
5. Norm referencing is a system by which the number of grades awarded at each level is largely fixed as a percentage of the overall participants in the exam. For example, although some adjustments are made year by year, there are always between 25% and 28% of pupils awarded a 'fail' grade in each GCSE subject area.
6. Andy Phippen and Louisa Street, *Online Resilience and Wellbeing in Young People*. Pub Palgrave Macmillan, 2002.

# Index

Anti-Bullying Alliance 52

Bates, Adele 18
Berry, Dr Jill 56
Bilton, Mary 5n2
Black Eyed Peas, The 21
Black, Paul 17, 96, 121
Brailsford, Dave 17
Brown, Brené 11

Campbell, Ross 22
Chapman, Gary 22
CHConline.org 32
cognitive behaviour therapy 11
Curran, Dr Andrew 21

Dix, Paul 42, 48
Dweck, Carol 17

Equality Act 39, 69, 125, 142
Essity 20

Foulkes, Lucy 29
Freedman, Sam 79
Fritz, Robert 12

Gamble, Jim 93
General Data Protection Regulations (GDPR) 70, 114, 142
Girls on Board 33, 34, 42, 51, 116, 144

Hattie, John 79

KCSiE 36, 37, 50

Lepkowska, Dorothy 119

Marinucci, Dr Alexandra 31
Marks, Gemma 31
McGregor, Douglas 61
Mill, John Stuart 29

National Careers Service 12
Nightingale, Julie 119

Phippen, Andy 27, 30, 152
Pink, Dan 150
Plato 125
PSHE Association 31

Quinn, Robert 56

Ringrose, Jessica 51
Riordan, Sally 79

SEND 6, 32, 36, 39, 85, 101, 120
Sherrington, Tom 100
Simpsons, The 5n1
Street, Louise 27, 30

Wellbeing Hub, The 31
William, Dylan 17, 96, 121
Wiseman, Rosalind 33
*Working with Boys* 34, 42, 52, 144

Young Minds 31

For Product Safety Concerns and Information please contact our EU representative GPSR@taylorandfrancis.com
Taylor & Francis Verlag GmbH, Kaufingerstraße 24, 80331 München, Germany

www.ingramcontent.com/pod-product-compliance
Lightning Source LLC
Chambersburg PA
CBHW082101230426
43670CB00017B/2912